3D Graphics with XNA Game Studio 4.0

Create attractive 3D graphics and visuals in your XNA games

Sean James

PUBLISHING

BIRMINGHAM - MUMBAI

3D Graphics with XNA Game Studio 4.0

First published: December 2010

Production Reference: 1071210

Published by Packt Publishing Ltd.
32 Lincoln Road
Olton
Birmingham, B27 6PA, UK.

ISBN 978-1-849690-04-1

www.packtpub.com

Cover Image by Charwak A (charwak86@gmail.com)

Credits

Author
Sean James

Reviewers
Zhenyu George Li
Cătălin Zima-Zegreanu

Acquisition Editor
David Barnes

Development Editor
Tariq Rakhange

Technical Editor
Namita Sahni

Copy Editor
Laxmi Subramanian

Indexers
Monica Ajmera Mehta
Rekha Nair

Editorial Team Leader
Aditya Belpathak

Project Team Leader
Ashwin Shetty

Project Coordinator
Poorvi Nair

Proofreader
Lynda Sliwoski

Graphics
Geetanjali Sawant

Production Coordinator
Shantanu Zagade

Cover Work
Shantanu Zagade

About the Author

Sean James is a computer science student who has been programming for many years. He started with web designing, learning HTML, PHP, JavaScript, and so on. Since then he has created many websites including his personal XNA and game development focused blog, www.innovativegames.net. In addition to web designing, he has interests in desktop software development and development for mobile devices such as Android, Windows Mobile, and Zune. However, his passion is for game development with DirectX, OpenGL, and XNA. Sean James lives in Claremont, CA with his family and two dogs.

I would like to thank my family and friends who supported me throughout the writing of this book, and all the people at Packt Publishing who worked hard on the book to support me. I would also like to thank the XNA community for providing such amazing resources, without which this book would not have been possible.

About the Reviewers

Zhenyu George Li has been working as a software engineer in the game industry for more than ten years. In his early years, George really enjoyed playing video games and dreamed to be a game developer, so he started learning Turbo C 3D programming and DirectX6 in 1998. George's article series, *The Road to Game Development – DirectX Programming with C++ Builder*, was published in the magazine *Computer Programming Techniques and Maintenance* in China in 2000, and George won the magazine's Best Writer prize of the year. After moving to Canada in 2001, George has been working for some companies on several game titles and tools such as CT Baseball (Taiwan), The Bigs2, Dead Rising 2, online poker games, Heroes of Mythology, Battle of Britain, and Avatar XNA skinned Model Animation Engine. As a video game developer, George has accumulated ample knowledge and experience in computer graphics, game play, game frontend and UI, as well as game engine and tools development.

The first time George used Microsoft XNA in 2005, he realized that XNA had great potential for developers, educators, and learners because of its easy-to-learn programming language, C#, and multi-platform support. In 2007, George's book *XNA PC and Xbox360 C# Game Programming* was published in Taiwan and promoted by Microsoft Taiwan. George was also invited to translate the book *Game Programming Gems 4* that was published in Taiwan in 2006.

I am thankful to Pat McGee for helping me with the Avatar XNA Skinned Mesh Animation Engine project and referring the opportunity of being the technical reviewer of *3D Graphics with XNA Game Studio 4.0*. I also want to appreciate Charles Yeh and Dr. Wyn Roberts' support on my works and publications.

Cătălin Zima-Zegreanu has been coding games and graphics as a hobby for over eight years, and is planning on continuing to do so. Starting with Pascal, he continued with OpenGl and DirectX and is now passionately in love with XNA Game Studio.

He got involved with XNA and its community since the first beta version, released back in 2006, and likes to hang around the official Creator's Club Forums, to chime in whenever he feels he can help someone. His activity as well as his articles and samples released for the growing community were rewarded with the Microsoft XNA/DirectX MVP Award. You can follow his activity on his own site (`http://catalinzima.com`), as well as on "Sgt. Conker" (`http://sgtconker.com`)—an XNA community site he's managing together with a group of "absolutely fine" men.

I'd like to thank my wife for being a geek. Just like me! :)

---

www.PacktPub.com

Support files, eBooks, discount offers and more

You might want to visit www.PacktPub.com for support files and downloads related to your book.

Did you know that Packt offers eBook versions of every book published, with PDF and ePub files available? You can upgrade to the eBook version at www.PacktPub.com and as a print book customer, you are entitled to a discount on the eBook copy. Get in touch with us at service@packtpub.com for more details.

At www.PacktPub.com, you can also read a collection of free technical articles, sign up for a range of free newsletters and receive exclusive discounts and offers on Packt books and eBooks.

http://PacktLib.PacktPub.com

Do you need instant solutions to your IT questions? PacktLib is Packt's online digital book library. Here, you can access, read and search across Packt's entire library of books.

Why Subscribe?

- Fully searchable across every book published by Packt
- Copy and paste, print and bookmark content
- On demand and accessible via web browser

Free Access for Packt account holders

If you have an account with Packt at www.PacktPub.com, you can use this to access PacktLib today and view nine entirely free books. Simply use your login credentials for immediate access.

Table of Contents

Preface

XNA is a very powerful API using which it's easy to make great games, especially when you have dazzling 3D effects. This book will show you how to implement the same 3D graphics used in professional games to make your games shine, and get those gamers addicted! This book will show you, step-by-step, how to implement the effects used in professional 3D games in your XNA games. Upon reaching the end of the book, you would have built an extensible framework for both basic 3D rendering and advanced effects. The one thing that can make or break a game is its appearance; players will mostly be attracted to a game if it looks good. One of the most common stopping points in an XNA game is its graphics, and many independent developers are not sure of how to implement the graphical effects needed to make great looking games. This book will help you avoid this pitfall, by walking you through the implementation of many common effects and graphics techniques used in professional games so that you can make your games look great.

What this book covers

Chapter 1, Getting Started with 3D, introduces the fundamentals of 3D graphics, including coordinate systems, matrices, and so on, which will be used for the rest of the book. We start by learning some simple model drawing code and finish by building a framework to implement a number of camera types. We also take a look at view frustum culling and how it can speed up our game.

Chapter 2, Introduction to HLSL, continues on the first chapter, explaining the graphics pipeline and shaders. We then look at a number of lighting and texturing effects, expanding on the framework built in Chapter 1 and adding a system that will allows us to draw our models with any effect.

Chapter 3, Advanced Lighting, continues our discussion of lighting, implementing more light types. We then look at several ways to increase the number of lights we can draw in a scene at a time.

Chapter 4, Projection and Shadowing Effects, builds on top of the renderer completed in Chapter 3 by adding two new effects: projected textures and shadow mapping.

Chapter 5, Shader Effects, takes a look at some "shader effects" such as normal mapping and reflections. We build a number of useful effects in this chapter such as a sky box and reflective water effect.

Chapter 6, Billboard and Particle Effects, investigates particle and billboarding effects—two effects that take advantage of 2D textures to create some interesting effects in 3D scenes such as foliage, clouds, and efficient trees and particle systems.

Chapter 7, Environmental Effects, discusses several "environmental" effects such as terrain, randomly "grown" foliage, and more. The chapter finishes by combining many effects created in the book thus far to create a spectacular mountainous terrain scene.

Chapter 8, Advanced Materials and Post Processing, expands on the material system created in the earlier chapter to allow for more advanced material types. It then takes a look at "post processing" effects like blurs, glows, and depth of field.

Chapter 9, Animation, takes a look at several different types of animation, including objects animation, keyframed animation, and skinned animation to introduce movement into our scenes.

What you need for this book

All you need for this book is XNA and Visual Studio—the whole list and guide is available at `creators.xna.com`.

Who this book is for

This book is mainly written for those who are familiar with object-oriented programming and C# and who are interested in improving the visual appearance of their XNA games. This book will be useful as a learning material for those who are new to graphics and for those who are looking to expand their toolset. Also, it can be used by game developers looking for an implementation guide or reference for effects or techniques they are already familiar with.

Conventions

In this book, you will find a number of styles of text that distinguish between different kinds of information. Here are some examples of these styles, and an explanation of their meaning.

Code words in text are shown as follows: "Next, we'll add a function to the `CModel` class that will allow us to set a given effect to any given mesh part".

A block of code is set as follows:

```
Effect lit = Content.Load<Effect>("LightingEffect");
Effect normal = Content.Load<Effect>("NormalMapEffect");

LightingMaterial marble = new LightingMaterial();
marble.SpecularColor = Color.White.ToVector3();
```

When we wish to draw your attention to a particular part of a code block, the relevant lines or items are set in bold:

```
technique Technique1
{
    pass p0
    {
        PixelShader = compile ps_2_0 PixelShaderFunction();
    }
}
```

New terms and **important words** are shown in bold. Words that you see on the screen, in menus or dialog boxes for example, appear in the text like this: "Then, choose **Image | Adjustments | Desaturate** to remove the color from the image."

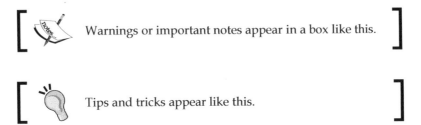

[Warnings or important notes appear in a box like this.]

[Tips and tricks appear like this.]

Reader feedback

Feedback from our readers is always welcome. Let us know what you think about this book—what you liked or may have disliked. Reader feedback is important for us to develop titles that you really get the most out of.

To send us general feedback, simply send an e-mail to `feedback@packtpub.com`, and mention the book title via the subject of your message.

If there is a book that you need and would like to see us publish, please send us a note in the **SUGGEST A TITLE** form on `www.packtpub.com` or e-mail `suggest@packtpub.com`.

If there is a topic that you have expertise in and you are interested in either writing or contributing to a book, see our author guide on `www.packtpub.com/authors`.

Customer support

Now that you are the proud owner of a Packt book, we have a number of things to help you to get the most from your purchase.

Downloading the example code for this book

You can download the example code files for all Packt books you have purchased from your account at `http://www.PacktPub.com`. If you purchased this book elsewhere, you can visit `http://www.PacktPub.com/support` and register to have the files e-mailed directly to you.

Errata

Although we have taken every care to ensure the accuracy of our content, mistakes do happen. If you find a mistake in one of our books—maybe a mistake in the text or the code—we would be grateful if you would report this to us. By doing so, you can save other readers from frustration and help us improve subsequent versions of this book. If you find any errata, please report them by visiting `http://www.packtpub.com/support`, selecting your book, clicking on the **errata submission form** link, and entering the details of your errata. Once your errata are verified, your submission will be accepted and the errata will be uploaded on our website, or added to any list of existing errata, under the Errata section of that title. Any existing errata can be viewed by selecting your title from `http://www.packtpub.com/support`.

Piracy

Piracy of copyrighted material on the Internet is an ongoing problem across all media. At Packt, we take the protection of our copyright and licenses very seriously. If you come across any illegal copies of our works, in any form, on the Internet, please provide us with the location address or website name immediately so that we can pursue a remedy.

Please contact us at copyright@packtpub.com with a link to the suspected pirated material.

We appreciate your help in protecting our authors, and our ability to bring you valuable content.

Questions

You can contact us at questions@packtpub.com if you are having a problem with any aspect of the book, and we will do our best to address it.

1

Getting Started with 3D

This chapter will provide you with a brief overview of the fundamentals of 3D graphics. We will create a number of useful classes and systems that will make work easier later on and provide us with a flexible framework for building games. This chapter will focus mainly on models, how they work, and how to view them with cameras. We will build a number of different types of camera that can be used in many situations we may encounter while building games. Next, we will look at a way to improve performance with a "view frustum culling" system, and finally, we'll build a small game that allows the player to fly a spaceship using keyboard controls.

Setting up a new project

The first step in any game is to set up the XNA game project in Visual Studio.

1. To begin with, ensure that XNA and Visual Studio are installed by following the guide available at `creators.xna.com` and launch Visual Studio. Once it has loaded, create a new project:

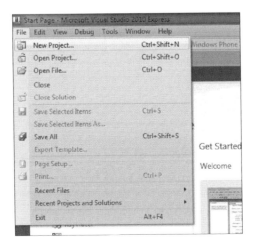

2. From the left-hand side, choose the version of XNA you want to work with. Generally, you should pick the most recent version available, unless you are specifically targeting an older version. If you've just installed XNA, there will be only one version of XNA to choose from. At the time of this writing, the most recent version was XNA 3.1. From the box on the right, specify that you want to create a **Windows Game**, and give it a name:

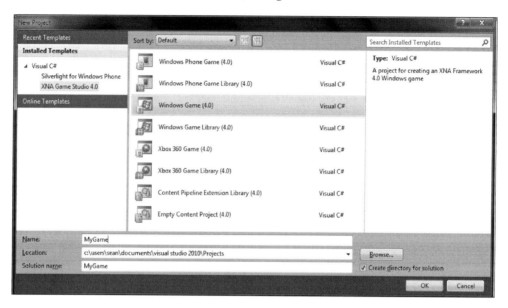

3. Click on **OK**, and you will be taken to the main file of the game project called `Game1.cs`. XNA will have created this file and added it to your project automatically. The `Game1` class is the main class in an XNA game. By default, this class is automatically instantiated when the game is loaded, and its member functions will be called automatically when they should perform their respective tasks.

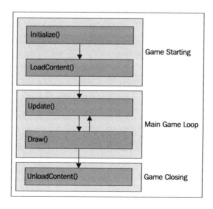

The automatically generated Game1 class contains a lot of excess comments and code, so once you have familiarized yourself with the class and its functions, simplify it to the following:

```
public class Game1 : Microsoft.Xna.Framework.Game
{
    GraphicsDeviceManager graphics;
    SpriteBatch spriteBatch;

    public Game1()
    {
      graphics = new GraphicsDeviceManager(this);
      Content.RootDirectory = "Content";
    }

    // Called when the game should load its content
    protected override void LoadContent()
    {
    }

    // Called when the game should update itself
    protected override void Update(GameTime gameTime)
    {
       base.Update(gameTime);
    }

    // Called when the game should draw itself
    protected override void Draw(GameTime gameTime)
    {
       GraphicsDevice.Clear(Color.CornflowerBlue);

       base.Draw(gameTime);
    }
}
```

The 3D coordinate system

One thing that all 3D systems hold in common is a **coordinate system**. Coordinate systems are important because they allow us to represent points in 3D space in a consistent manner as distances from a center point called the **origin** along a number of axes. You're probably used to the idea of a 2D coordinate system from your math classes in school—the origin was at (0, 0) and the X and Y axes grew to the right and up respectively. A 3D coordinate system is very similar, except for the addition of a third axis labeled the **Z-axis**. XNA uses what is called a "right-handed" coordinate system, meaning that the X and Y axes grow the way you're used to (to the right and up respectively), and the Z-axis grows "towards" you. If the X and Y axes were placed flat on your computer screen, you can imagine the Z-axis as growing out of the screen towards you.

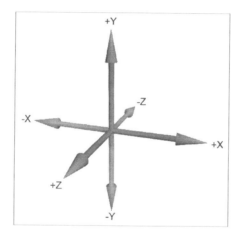

With this coordinate system, we can define points in space. For example, let's assume that our coordinate system uses meters as units. Say for a moment, we were sitting at the origin (0, 0, 0) and were facing down the negative portion of the Z-axis. If we wanted to note the location of an object sitting five meters in front of us, three meters to the right, on a table one meter tall, we would say that the object was at (3, 1, -5).

Matrices

Matrices are mathematical structures that are used in 3D graphics to represent **transformations**—operations performed on a point to move it in some way. The three common transformations are translation (movement), rotation, and scaling (changing size). When a transformation is applied to a model, each vertex in the model is multiplied by the transformation's matrix until the entire model has been transformed.

Matrices can be combined by multiplying them together. It is worth noting that matrix multiplication is done from right to left, so the last matrix to be multiplied will be the first to affect the model and so on. This means that rotating and then moving a model will not have the same effect as moving and then rotating it. Generally, unless you mean to do otherwise, the matrices should be multiplied in the following order: *scaling * rotation * transformation*.

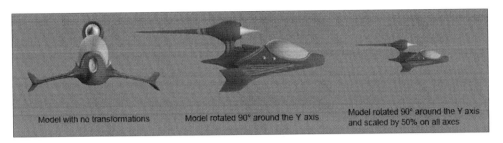

Model with no transformations   Model rotated 90° around the Y axis   Model rotated 90° around the Y axis and scaled by 50% on all axes

In the 3D graphics world, there are usually three matrices that must be calculated to draw an object onto the screen: the **world**, **view**, and **projection** matrices. The **world matrix** is the result of all of our transformation matrices multiplied together. Once this transformation has been applied, the model has moved from what is called "local" or "object space" to "world space". Each model in a scene has a different world matrix, as they all have different locations, orientations, and so on. It is also possible that each "piece" of a model (or **mesh**) may have its own world matrix. For example, the head and leg of a human model will likely have their own matrices to offset them from the center of the model (its **root**). When the model is drawn, each mesh has its transformation multiplied by the entire model's world matrix to calculate the final world matrix.

The **view matrix** is used to transform the scene from world space into *view space*: the world as seen by the camera. The world matrix for each model is simply multiplied by the view matrix to transform the scene. The projection matrix then transforms the three-dimensional position of each vertex in the scene into the two-dimensional projection of the scene that is drawn onto the screen. When the 3D world/view matrix combination is multiplied by the projection matrix, the scene is flattened out so that it can be drawn onto a 2D screen.

Loading a model

A **model** is a file exported from a 3D modeling package such as 3D Studio Max or Blender. The file basically contains a list of points called **vertices**, which form the edges of polygons that, joined together, give the appearance of a smooth surface:

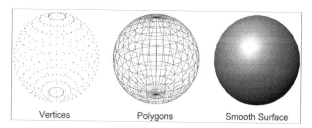

Vertices   Polygons   Smooth Surface

To load a model, we must add it to our game's content project. XNA will automatically build all of the content in our content project so that we can use it in our game. To add a model to the content project, open the **Solution Explorer**, right-click on the content project (labeled **Content**), and click on **Add Existing Item**.

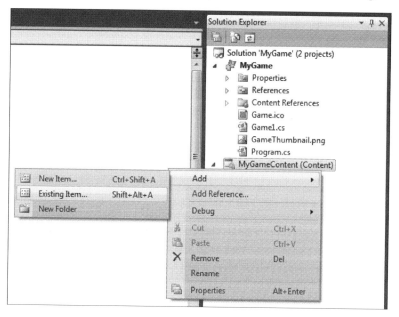

In addition to building all of the content in the content project, XNA builds any files referenced by a piece of content. Because our model references its texture, we need to exclude the texture from the list of content to build or it will be built twice. Right-click on the texture and then select **Exclude From Project**. This will remove the texture from the content project but will not delete the file itself, which will allow XNA to find it when building the model but still only build it once.

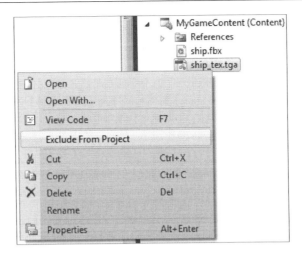

Now that the content pipeline is building our model for us, we can load it into our game. We do this with the ContentManager class—a class used to access the runtime functionality of the content pipeline. The Game class already has an instance of the ContentManager class built-in, so we can go ahead and use it in the LoadContent() method.

First, an instance of the Model class will be needed. The Model class contains all the data necessary to draw and work with a model. We will also need an array of matrices representing the model's built-in mesh transformations. Add the following member definitions:

```
Model model;
Matrix[] transforms;
```

Now, in the LoadContent() method, we can use the ContentManager to load the model. The Load() function of the ContentManager class takes the name of the resource to load—the original filename without its extension. Note that this means we can't have multiple files with the same name only varying by extension.

```
model = Content.Load<Model>("ship");

transforms = new Matrix[model.Bones.Count];
model.CopyAbsoluteBoneTransformsTo(transforms);
```

In XNA, a model is made up of pieces called **meshes**. As described earlier, each model has its own transformation in 3D space, and each mesh also has its own transformation relative to the model's transformation as a whole. The Model class stores these transformations as a skeleton structure with each mesh attached to a bone. The last two lines in the previous code snippet copied that skeleton into the transforms array.

Drawing a model

Now that the model has been loaded, we are ready to draw it. We do this in the `Draw()` function of our game. Games redraw dozens of times per second, and each redraw is called a **frame**. We need to clear the screen before drawing a new frame, and we do so using XNA's `GraphicsDevice.Clear()` function. The single argument allows us to change the color to which the screen is cleared:

```
GraphicsDevice.Clear(Color.CornflowerBlue);
```

The first step of drawing the model itself is to calculate the view and projection matrices. To calculate the view matrix, we will use the `CreateLookAt()` static function of the `Matrix` class, which accepts as arguments a camera position, target, and up direction. The **position** is simply where in 3D space the camera should be placed, the **target** is the point the camera should be looking at, and the **up** vector is literally the direction that is "up" relative to the camera position. This code will go in the `Draw()` function after the `GraphicsDevice` is cleared:

```
Matrix view = Matrix.CreateLookAt(
    new Vector3(200, 300, 900),
    new Vector3(0, 50, 0),
    Vector3.Up);
```

There are some exceptions, but usually we calculate the projection matrix using the `Matrix` class' `CreatePerspectiveFieldOfView()` function, which accepts, in order, a field of view (in radians), the aspect ratio, and the near and far plane distances. These values define the shape of the view frustum as seen in the following figure. It is used to decide which objects and vertices are onscreen and which are not when drawing, and how to squish the scene down to fit onto the two-dimensional screen.

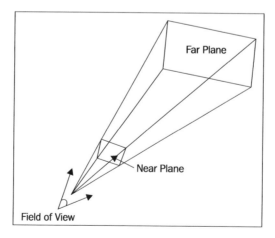

The near plane and far plane determine the distances at which objects will start and stop being drawn. Outside of the range between the two planes, objects will be **clipped**—meaning they will not be drawn. The field of view determines how "wide" the area seen by the camera is. Most first person shooters use an angle between 45 and 60 degrees for their field of view as anything beyond that range would start to distort the scene. A fish eye lens, on the other hand, would have a field of view closer to 180 degrees. This allows it to see more of the scene without moving, but it also distorts the scene at the edges. 45 degrees is a good starting point as it matches human vision closest without warping the image. The final value, the **aspect ratio**, is calculated by dividing the width of the screen by the height of the screen, and is used by the `CreatePerspectiveFieldOfView()` function to determine the "shape" of the screen in regards to its width and height. The `GraphicsDevice` has a precalculated aspect ratio value available that we can use when calculating the projection matrix:

```
Matrix projection = Matrix.CreatePerspectiveFieldOfView(
    MathHelper.ToRadians(45), GraphicsDevice.Viewport.AspectRatio,
    0.1f, 10000.0f);
```

The last matrix needed to draw the model is the world matrix. However, as discussed earlier, each mesh in the model has its own transformation relative to the model's overall transformation. This means that we will need to calculate a world matrix for each mesh. We'll start with the overall transformation and add the transformations from the `modelTransformations` array per mesh. Each mesh also has what is called an **effect**. We will look at effects in much more depth in the coming chapters, but for now, just remember that they are used to determine the appearance of a model. We will be using one of XNA's built-in effects (called **BasicEffect**) for now, so all we need to do is set its `World`, `View`, and `Projection` properties:

```
// Calculate the starting world matrix
Matrix baseWorld = Matrix.CreateScale(0.4f) *
    Matrix.CreateRotationY(MathHelper.ToRadians(180));

foreach (ModelMesh mesh in model.Meshes)
{
    // Calculate each mesh's world matrix
    Matrix localWorld = modelTransforms[mesh.ParentBone.Index]
        * baseWorld;

    foreach (ModelMeshPart part in mesh.MeshParts)
    {
        BasicEffect e = (BasicEffect)part.Effect;

        // Set the world, view, and projection matrices to the effect
        e.World = localWorld;
```

```
            e.View = view;
            e.Projection = projection;

            e.EnableDefaultLighting();
        }

    // Draw the mesh
    mesh.Draw();
    }
```

XNA will already have added the last piece of code for you as well, but it is important to ensure that this code is still in place at the end of the Draw() function. This line of code simply calls the Draw() function of the base Game class, ensuring that the game runs correctly.

```
    base.Draw(gameTime);
```

The complete code for the Game1 class is now as follows:

```
public class Game1 : Microsoft.Xna.Framework.Game
{
    GraphicsDeviceManager graphics;
    SpriteBatch spriteBatch;

    Model model;
    Matrix[] modelTransforms;

    public Game1()
    {
        graphics = new GraphicsDeviceManager(this);
        Content.RootDirectory = "Content";

        graphics.PreferredBackBufferWidth = 1280;
        graphics.PreferredBackBufferHeight = 800;
    }

    // Called when the game should load its content
    protected override void LoadContent()
    {
        spriteBatch = new SpriteBatch(GraphicsDevice);

        model = Content.Load<Model>("ship");

        modelTransforms = new Matrix[model.Bones.Count];
        model.CopyAbsoluteBoneTransformsTo(modelTransforms);
```

```
}

// Called when the game should update itself
protected override void Update(GameTime gameTime)
{
    base.Update(gameTime);
}

// Called when the game should draw itself
protected override void Draw(GameTime gameTime)
{
    GraphicsDevice.Clear(Color.CornflowerBlue);

    Matrix view = Matrix.CreateLookAt(
            new Vector3(200, 300, 900),
            new Vector3(0, 50, 0),
            Vector3.Up);

    Matrix projection = Matrix.CreatePerspectiveFieldOfView(
        MathHelper.ToRadians(45),
        GraphicsDevice.Viewport.AspectRatio,
        0.1f, 10000.0f);

    // Calculate the starting world matrix
    Matrix baseWorld = Matrix.CreateScale(0.4f) *
        Matrix.CreateRotationY(MathHelper.ToRadians(180));

    foreach (ModelMesh mesh in model.Meshes)
    {
        // Calculate each mesh's world matrix
        Matrix localWorld = modelTransforms[mesh.ParentBone.Index]
            * baseWorld;

        foreach (ModelMeshPart part in mesh.MeshParts)
        {
            BasicEffect e = (BasicEffect)part.Effect;

            // Set the world, view, and projection
            // matrices to the effect
            e.World = localWorld;
            e.View = view;
            e.Projection = projection;

            e.EnableDefaultLighting();
        }
```

```
            // Draw the mesh
        mesh.Draw();
    }

    base.Draw(gameTime);
    }
}
```

Run the game (**Debug | Start Debugging,** or *F5*) and you should see our spaceship in all its glory:

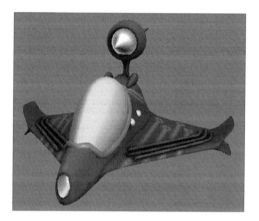

Creating a Custom Model class

The previous code works for drawing one model, but what if we wanted to draw more than one? More than ten? Writing the previous code out for each model would quickly become unmanageable. To make our lives a little easier, we'll take the previous code and put it into a new class called CModel (for custom model). This class will handle loading the transformations from a model, setting the matrices to the mesh part effects, and so on. Later on, it will handle setting custom effects, manage textures, and more. For now, we will keep it simple:

```
public class CModel
{
    public Vector3 Position { get; set; }
    public Vector3 Rotation { get; set; }
    public Vector3 Scale { get; set; }

    public Model Model { get; private set; }
    private Matrix[] modelTransforms;

    private GraphicsDevice graphicsDevice;
```

```
public CModel(Model Model, Vector3 Position, Vector3 Rotation,
    Vector3 Scale, GraphicsDevice graphicsDevice)
{
  this.Model = Model;

  modelTransforms = new Matrix[Model.Bones.Count];
  Model.CopyAbsoluteBoneTransformsTo(modelTransforms);

  this.Position = Position;
  this.Rotation = Rotation;
  this.Scale = Scale;

  this.graphicsDevice = graphicsDevice;
}

public void Draw(Matrix View, Matrix Projection)
{
    // Calculate the base transformation by combining
    // translation, rotation, and scaling
    Matrix baseWorld = Matrix.CreateScale(Scale)
        * Matrix.CreateFromYawPitchRoll(
          Rotation.Y, Rotation.X, Rotation.Z)
        * Matrix.CreateTranslation(Position);

    foreach (ModelMesh mesh in Model.Meshes)
    {
      Matrix localWorld = modelTransforms[mesh.ParentBone.Index]
        * baseWorld;

      foreach (ModelMeshPart meshPart in mesh.MeshParts)
      {
        BasicEffect effect = (BasicEffect)meshPart.Effect;

        effect.World = localWorld;
        effect.View = View;
        effect.Projection = Projection;

        effect.EnableDefaultLighting();
      }

      mesh.Draw();
    }
  }
}
```

We can now simplify the `Game1` class to draw a list of models:

```
GraphicsDeviceManager graphics;
SpriteBatch spriteBatch;

List<CModel> models = new List<CModel>();
```

As a demonstration, let's add nine copies of our spaceship to that list in the `LoadContent()` method:

```
for (int y = 0; y < 3; y++)
  for (int x = 0; x < 3; x++)
  {
    Vector3 position = new Vector3(
      -600 + x * 600, -400 + y * 400, 0);

    models.Add(new CModel(Content.Load<Model>("ship"), position,
            new Vector3(0, MathHelper.ToRadians(90) * (y * 3 + x), 0),
            new Vector3(0.25f), GraphicsDevice));
  }
```

We can now update our `Draw()` method to draw a list of models, then we can run the game and see the result:

```
// Called when the game should draw itself
protected override void Draw(GameTime gameTime)
{
  GraphicsDevice.Clear(Color.CornflowerBlue);

  Matrix view = Matrix.CreateLookAt(
        new Vector3(0, 300, 2000),
        new Vector3(0, 0, 0),
        Vector3.Up);

  Matrix projection = Matrix.CreatePerspectiveFieldOfView(
        MathHelper.ToRadians(45), GraphicsDevice.Viewport.AspectRatio,
        0.1f, 10000.0f);

  foreach (CModel model in models)
    model.Draw(view, projection);

  base.Draw(gameTime);
}
```

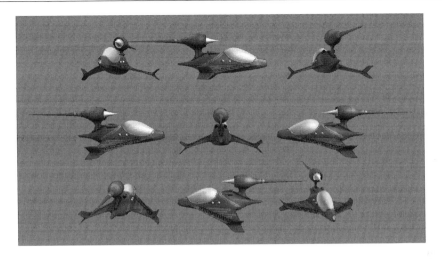

Creating a Camera class

Much like we did with the CModel class, let's create a reusable Camera class. We'll start with a base class that represents a camera at its lowest level: simply the view and projection matrices. We use a base class that all camera types will inherit from because we want to be able to use all camera types interchangeably. This Camera base class will also take care of calculating the projection matrix unless derived classes choose to do so themselves.

```
public abstract class Camera
{
  public Matrix View { get; set; }
  public Matrix Projection { get; set; }
  protected GraphicsDevice GraphicsDevice { get; set; }

  public Camera(GraphicsDevice graphicsDevice)
  {
     this.GraphicsDevice = graphicsDevice;
     generatePerspectiveProjectionMatrix(MathHelper.PiOver4);
  }

  private void generatePerspectiveProjectionMatrix(float FieldOfView)
  {
    PresentationParameters pp = GraphicsDevice.PresentationParameters;

    float aspectRatio = (float)pp.BackBufferWidth /
                        (float)pp.BackBufferHeight;
```

```
        this.Projection = Matrix.CreatePerspectiveFieldOfView(
            MathHelper.ToRadians(45), aspectRatio, 0.1f, 1000000.0f);
    }

    public virtual void Update()
    {
    }
}
```

Creating a target camera

Now that we have our base class, let's create the most basic type of camera — the **target camera**. This is simply a camera with two components — a position and a target. The camera points from the position towards the target, similar to the "camera" we used when we first drew our model:

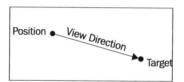

This data is more or less directly passed into the CreateLookAt() function in the Matrix class to calculate the view matrix. The call in the constructor to the Camera base class' constructor ensures that the projection matrix and other matrices are calculated for us:

```
public class TargetCamera : Camera
{
    public Vector3 Position { get; set; }
    public Vector3 Target { get; set; }

    public TargetCamera(Vector3 Position, Vector3 Target,
        GraphicsDevice graphicsDevice) : base(graphicsDevice)
    {
        this.Position = Position;
        this.Target = Target;
    }

    public override void Update()
    {
        Vector3 forward = Target - Position;
        Vector3 side = Vector3.Cross(forward, Vector3.Up);
        Vector3 up = Vector3.Cross(forward, side);
        this.View = Matrix.CreateLookAt(Position, Target, up);
    }
}
```

As you can see, the `Position` and `Target` values can be set freely through their public properties or through the constructor to position the camera any way desired at any time, as the `Update()` function will update the view matrix as necessary. We can now once again update the `Game1` class to use the `TargetCamera` instead of doing all the camera calculations itself. In addition to our list of models, we will also need a camera:

```
List<CModel> models = new List<CModel>();
Camera camera;
```

We will need to initialize the camera along with any models in the `LoadContent()` method:

```
models.Add(new CModel(Content.Load<Model>("ship"),
    Vector3.Zero, Vector3.Zero, new Vector3(0.6f), GraphicsDevice));

camera = new TargetCamera(
    new Vector3(300, 300, -1800),
    Vector3.Zero, GraphicsDevice);
```

We need to update.the camera in the `Update()` method:

```
// Called when the game should update itself
protected override void Update(GameTime gameTime)
{
   camera.Update();

   base.Update(gameTime);
}
```

Finally, we can use the `View` and `Projection` properties of `camera` in the `Draw()` method:

```
// Called when the game should draw itself
protected override void Draw(GameTime gameTime)
{
   GraphicsDevice.Clear(Color.CornflowerBlue);

   foreach (CModel model in models)
       model.Draw(camera.View, camera.Projection);

   base.Draw(gameTime);
}
```

We now have two classes, TargetCamera and CModel, which can be reused easily, and a base class for creating any type of camera we could need. We'll use the rest of this chapter to look at other types of cameras, and to add a system that will speed up the game by keeping it from drawing (culling) objects that are not in the camera's view.

Upgrading the camera to a free camera

At the moment, we can put our camera at one point and aim it at another. This works for a static scene, but it doesn't allow for any freedom in a real game. Most games would be pretty difficult to play if the camera can't move around, so this will be our next task. The free camera we will create will operate like those found in **First-Person-Shooter (FPS)** games, which allow the player to move around with the *W*, *S*, *A*, and *D* keys (for forward, back, left, and right respectively), and look around with the mouse. On the Xbox 360, we would use the left joystick for movement and the right joystick to rotate the camera.

```
public class FreeCamera : Camera
{
  public float Yaw { get; set; }
  public float Pitch { get; set; }

  public Vector3 Position { get; set; }
  public Vector3 Target { get; private set; }

  private Vector3 translation;

  public FreeCamera(Vector3 Position, float Yaw, float Pitch,
        GraphicsDevice graphicsDevice) : base(graphicsDevice)
  {
    this.Position = Position;
    this.Yaw = Yaw;
    this.Pitch = Pitch;

    translation = Vector3.Zero;
  }
}
```

The FreeCamera class adds two new values that the TargetCamera class didn't have—yaw and pitch. These two values (in radians) determine the amount that the camera has been rotated around the Y and X axes, respectively. The yaw and pitch values can be modified (usually based on mouse movements) through the new Rotate() method. There is also a new value called translation that accumulates the amount that the camera has moved (in the direction the camera is facing) between frames. The Move() function modifies this value (usually based on keyboard or joystick input):

```
public void Rotate(float YawChange, float PitchChange)
{
  this.Yaw += YawChange;
  this.Pitch += PitchChange;
}

public void Move(Vector3 Translation)
{
  this.translation += Translation;
}
```

The `Update()` function does the math to calculate the new view matrix:

```
public override void Update()
{
  // Calculate the rotation matrix
  Matrix rotation = Matrix.CreateFromYawPitchRoll(Yaw, Pitch, 0);

  // Offset the position and reset the translation
  translation = Vector3.Transform(translation, rotation);
  Position += translation;
  translation = Vector3.Zero;

  // Calculate the new target
  Vector3 forward = Vector3.Transform(Vector3.Forward, rotation);
  Target = Position + forward;

  // Calculate the up vector
  Vector3 up = Vector3.Transform(Vector3.Up, rotation);

  // Calculate the view matrix
  View = Matrix.CreateLookAt(Position, Target, up);
}
```

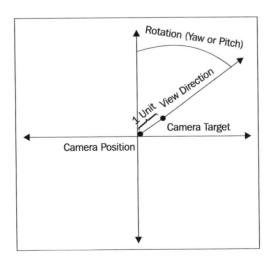

Once again we are ready to modify the Game1 class, this time to switch to our new camera and add keyboard and mouse control. First, we need to change the type of camera we are creating in the LoadContent() function:

```
camera = new FreeCamera(new Vector3(1000, 0, -2000),
    MathHelper.ToRadians(153), // Turned around 153 degrees
    MathHelper.ToRadians(5), // Pitched up 13 degrees
    GraphicsDevice);
```

Let's start by adding mouse control. In order to measure the amount of mouse movement between frames, we need to be able to store the last frame's mouse state. We can then compare that mouse state to the current mouse state. To store the last frame's mouse state, we will add a MouseState member variable:

```
List<CModel> models = new List<CModel>();
Camera camera;


MouseState lastMouseState;
```

This value needs to be initialized once before the Update method so that the game doesn't crash when trying to access it on the first frame, so we will grab the mouse state at the end of the LoadContent method:

```
lastMouseState = Mouse.GetState();
```

Now, we can create a new function that the Update() method will use to update the camera:

```
// Called when the game should update itself
protected override void Update(GameTime gameTime)
{
  updateCamera(gameTime);

  base.Update(gameTime);
}

void updateCamera(GameTime gameTime)
{
  // Get the new keyboard and mouse state
  MouseState mouseState = Mouse.GetState();
  KeyboardState keyState = Keyboard.GetState();

  // Determine how much the camera should turn
  float deltaX = (float)lastMouseState.X - (float)mouseState.X;
  float deltaY = (float)lastMouseState.Y - (float)mouseState.Y;

  // Rotate the camera
  ((FreeCamera)camera).Rotate(deltaX * .01f, deltaY * .01f);

  Vector3 translation = Vector3.Zero;
```

```
    // Determine in which direction to move the camera
    if (keyState.IsKeyDown(Keys.W)) translation += Vector3.Forward;
    if (keyState.IsKeyDown(Keys.S)) translation += Vector3.Backward;
    if (keyState.IsKeyDown(Keys.A)) translation += Vector3.Left;
    if (keyState.IsKeyDown(Keys.D)) translation += Vector3.Right;

    // Move 3 units per millisecond, independent of frame rate
    translation *= 3 * (float)gameTime.ElapsedGameTime.
    TotalMilliseconds;

    // Move the camera
    ((FreeCamera)camera).Move(translation);

    // Update the camera
    camera.Update();

    // Update the mouse state
    lastMouseState = mouseState;
}
```

Run the game again, and you should be able to move and rotate the camera with the mouse and *W*, *S*, *A*, and *D* keys.

Calculating bounding spheres for models

It is often convenient for us to have a simplified representation of the geometry of a model. Because complex models are made of hundreds if not thousands of vertices, it is often too inefficient to check for object intersection per vertex between every object in the scene when doing collision detection, for example. To simplify collision checks, we will use what is called a **bounding volume**, specifically a bounding sphere. Let's add some functionality to our CModel class to calculate bounding spheres for us. To start, we need to add a new BoundingSphere member variable to the CModel class:

```
private Matrix[] modelTransforms;
private GraphicsDevice graphicsDevice;
private BoundingSphere boundingSphere;
```

Next, we will create a function to calculate this bounding sphere based on our model's geometry:

```
private void buildBoundingSphere()
{
  BoundingSphere sphere = new BoundingSphere(Vector3.Zero, 0);

  // Merge all the model's built in bounding spheres
  foreach (ModelMesh mesh in Model.Meshes)
  {
    BoundingSphere transformed = mesh.BoundingSphere.Transform(
```

```
        modelTransforms[mesh.ParentBone.Index]);

      sphere = BoundingSphere.CreateMerged(sphere, transformed);
    }

    this.boundingSphere = sphere;
  }
```

We need to be sure to call this function in our constructor:

```
public CModel(Model Model, Vector3 Position, Vector3 Rotation,
    Vector3 Scale, GraphicsDevice graphicsDevice)
{
  this.Model = Model;

  modelTransforms = new Matrix[Model.Bones.Count];
  Model.CopyAbsoluteBoneTransformsTo(modelTransforms);

  buildBoundingSphere();


  ...
```

However, there is one problem with this approach: this bounding sphere is centered at the origin, so if we were to move our model, the bounding sphere would no longer contain the model. To solve this problem, we will add a public property that translates our origin-centered boundingSphere value to the model's current position and scales it based on our model's scale:

```
public BoundingSphere BoundingSphere
{
  get
  {
    // No need for rotation, as this is a sphere
    Matrix worldTransform = Matrix.CreateScale(Scale)
        * Matrix.CreateTranslation(Position);

    BoundingSphere transformed = boundingSphere;
    transformed = transformed.Transform(worldTransform);

    return transformed;
  }
}
```

View frustum culling

One usage of our new bounding sphere system is to determine which objects are onscreen. This is useful when, for example, we are drawing a large number of objects: if we first check whether an object is onscreen before drawing it, we have a chance of improving the performance of our games if some of the objects in the scene leave the player's view. This is called **view frustum culling** because we are checking if an object's bounding sphere intersects the view frustum, and if it doesn't, we cull it (refrain from drawing it). It is worth noting that this method of culling is not an all-encompassing method of optimization—if you are drawing many small objects, it may not be worth the time to cull objects because the graphics card won't process pixels that are offscreen anyway.

The first thing we need to do is to actually calculate a view frustum. We can do this very simply once we know our view and projection matrices. Let's go back to our abstract `Camera` class and add a `BoundingFrustum`. The `BoundingFrustum` class has a function to check if a `BoundingSphere` is in view.

```
public BoundingFrustum Frustum { get; private set; }
```

The view and projection matrices can change frequently, so we need to update the frustum whenever they change. We will do this by calling the `generateFrustum()` function that we will write shortly in the View and Projection properties' set accessors:

```
Matrix view;
Matrix projection;

public Matrix Projection
{
  get { return projection; }
  protected set
  {
    projection = value;
    generateFrustum();
  }
}

public Matrix View
{
  get { return view; }
  protected set
  {
    view = value;
    generateFrustum();
```

```
    }
  }

  private void generateFrustum()
  {
    Matrix viewProjection = View * Projection;
    Frustum = new BoundingFrustum(viewProjection);
  }
```

Finally, we will make things a little easier on ourselves by adding some shortcuts to check if bounding boxes and bounding spheres are visible. Because we are doing this in the base class, these functions will conveniently work for any camera type.

```
  public bool BoundingVolumeIsInView(BoundingSphere sphere)
  {
    return (Frustum.Contains(sphere) != ContainmentType.Disjoint);
  }

  public bool BoundingVolumeIsInView(BoundingBox box)
  {
    return (Frustum.Contains(box) != ContainmentType.Disjoint);
  }
```

Finally, we can update the Game1 class to use this new system. Our new Draw() function will check if the bounding sphere of each model to be drawn is in view, and if so, it will draw the model. If it doesn't end up drawing any models, it will clear the screen to red so we can tell if models are being culled correctly:

```
  // Called when the game should draw itself
  protected override void Draw(GameTime gameTime)
  {
    GraphicsDevice.Clear(Color.CornflowerBlue);

    int nModelsDrawn = 0;

    foreach (CModel model in models)
      if (camera.BoundingVolumeIsInView(model.BoundingSphere))
      {
        nModelsDrawn++;
        model.Draw(camera.View, camera.Projection);
      }

    if (nModelsDrawn == 0)
      GraphicsDevice.Clear(Color.Red);

    base.Draw(gameTime);
  }
```

Once you have tried this out and are convinced this system works, feel free to remove the extra code that clears the screen to red:

```
// Called when the game should draw itself
protected override void Draw(GameTime gameTime)
{
  GraphicsDevice.Clear(Color.CornflowerBlue);

  foreach (CModel model in models)
    if (camera.BoundingVolumeIsInView(model.BoundingSphere))
        model.Draw(camera.View, camera.Projection);

  base.Draw(gameTime);
}
```

Additional camera types: Arc-Ball

We will spend the rest of this chapter looking at two other camera types, and finally at the end we will use one of them to build a small game where the player gets to fly the spaceship that we've been looking at thus far around. The first camera type is the **Arc-Ball camera**.

An Arc-Ball camera is essentially the opposite of a free camera. Instead of sitting at a point and looking at a target, the target sits at one point and the camera rotates around it. As an example, this type of camera is commonly used when editing the appearance of a vehicle or character in a 3D game. The camera is free to "float around" the object, but it can't turn around or leave the object, as the target of the camera is at the center of the sphere the camera is allowed to travel on.

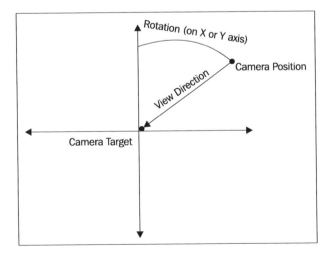

Most games limit the vertical and zoom range of this type of camera, so our camera will allow this as well. The code for the ArcBall Camera class is as follows:

```
public class ArcBallCamera : Camera
{
  // Rotation around the two axes
  public float RotationX { get; set; }
  public float RotationY { get; set; }

  // Y axis rotation limits (radians)
  public float MinRotationY { get; set; }
  public float MaxRotationY { get; set; }

  // Distance between the target and camera
  public float Distance { get; set; }

  // Distance limits
  public float MinDistance { get; set; }
  public float MaxDistance { get; set; }

  // Calculated position and specified target
  public Vector3 Position { get; private set; }
  public Vector3 Target { get; set; }

  public ArcBallCamera(Vector3 Target, float RotationX,
    float RotationY, float MinRotationY, float MaxRotationY,
    float Distance, float MinDistance, float MaxDistance,
    GraphicsDevice graphicsDevice) : base(graphicsDevice)
    {
      this.Target = Target;

      this.MinRotationY = MinRotationY;
      this.MaxRotationY = MaxRotationY;

      // Lock the y axis rotation between the min and max values
      this.RotationY = MathHelper.Clamp(RotationY, MinRotationY,
      MaxRotationY);

      this.RotationX = RotationX;

      this.MinDistance = MinDistance;
      this.MaxDistance = MaxDistance;

      // Lock the distance between the min and max values
```

```
            this.Distance = MathHelper.Clamp(Distance, MinDistance,
            MaxDistance);
        }

    public void Move(float DistanceChange)
    {
        this.Distance += DistanceChange;

        this.Distance = MathHelper.Clamp(Distance, MinDistance,
        MaxDistance);
    }

    public void Rotate(float RotationXChange, float RotationYChange)
    {
        this.RotationX += RotationXChange;
        this.RotationY += -RotationYChange;

        this.RotationY = MathHelper.Clamp(RotationY, MinRotationY,
        MaxRotationY);
    }

    public void Translate(Vector3 PositionChange)
    {
        this.Position += PositionChange;
    }

    public override void Update()
    {
        // Calculate rotation matrix from rotation values
        Matrix rotation = Matrix.CreateFromYawPitchRoll(RotationX, -
        RotationY, 0);

        // Translate down the Z axis by the desired distance
        // between the camera and object, then rotate that
        // vector to find the camera offset from the target
        Vector3 translation = new Vector3(0, 0, Distance);
        translation = Vector3.Transform(translation, rotation);

        Position = Target + translation;

        // Calculate the up vector from the rotation matrix
        Vector3 up = Vector3.Transform(Vector3.Up, rotation);

        View = Matrix.CreateLookAt(Position, Target, up);
    }
}
```

To implement this camera in the `Game1` class, we first instantiate our camera as an `ArcBallCamera` in the `LoadContent()` method:

```
camera = new ArcBallCamera(Vector3.Zero, 0, 0, 0, MathHelper.PiOver2,
            1200, 1000, 2000, GraphicsDevice);
```

Second, we need to update the `updateCamera()` function to reflect the way this new camera type moves:

```
void updateCamera(GameTime gameTime)
{
  // Get the new keyboard and mouse state
  MouseState mouseState = Mouse.GetState();
  KeyboardState keyState = Keyboard.GetState();

  // Determine how much the camera should turn
  float deltaX = (float)lastMouseState.X - (float)mouseState.X;
  float deltaY = (float)lastMouseState.Y - (float)mouseState.Y;

  // Rotate the camera
  ((ArcBallCamera)camera).Rotate(deltaX * .01f, deltaY * .01f);

  // Calculate scroll wheel movement
  float scrollDelta = (float)lastMouseState.ScrollWheelValue -
    (float)mouseState.ScrollWheelValue;

  // Move the camera
  ((ArcBallCamera)camera).Move(scrollDelta);

  // Update the camera
  camera.Update();

  // Update the mouse state
  lastMouseState = mouseState;
}
```

Run the game, and you will be able to rotate around the ship with the mouse, and move towards and away from it with the scroll wheel.

Additional camera types: chase camera

The last camera type we will look at is the chase camera. A **chase camera** is designed to "chase" an object. Generally, the camera follows the object at some distance and turns with it. This is the type of camera used, for example, in most third person situations—racing games, third person shooters, flight simulators, and so on. The chase distance and view direction are generally determined using an offset for the camera position and an offset for the target position from the object's position. The view matrix is then calculated as usual based on those values.

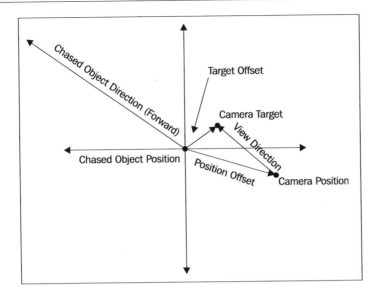

In this case, the chase camera also has a relative rotation value that allows the camera to rotate independently of the object, and a "springiness" value that allows the camera to "bend" from side-to-side instead of rigidly following the object. This can create more of a feeling of movement than simply following the object because the camera responds more like it would under real-life physics. The code for the `ChaseCamera` class is as shown:

```
public class ChaseCamera : Camera
{
  public Vector3 Position { get; private set; }
  public Vector3 Target { get; private set; }

  public Vector3 FollowTargetPosition { get; private set; }
  public Vector3 FollowTargetRotation { get; private set; }

  public Vector3 PositionOffset { get; set; }
  public Vector3 TargetOffset { get; set; }

  public Vector3 RelativeCameraRotation { get; set; }

    float springiness = .15f;

  public float Springiness
  {
    get { return springiness; }
    set { springiness = MathHelper.Clamp(value, 0, 1); }
  }

  public ChaseCamera(Vector3 PositionOffset, Vector3 TargetOffset,
      Vector3 RelativeCameraRotation, GraphicsDevice graphicsDevice)
      : base(graphicsDevice)
```

```
    {
        this.PositionOffset = PositionOffset;
        this.TargetOffset = TargetOffset;
        this.RelativeCameraRotation = RelativeCameraRotation;
    }

    public void Move(Vector3 NewFollowTargetPosition,
        Vector3 NewFollowTargetRotation)
    {
        this.FollowTargetPosition = NewFollowTargetPosition;
        this.FollowTargetRotation = NewFollowTargetRotation;
    }

    public void Rotate(Vector3 RotationChange)
    {
        this.RelativeCameraRotation += RotationChange;
    }

    public override void Update()
    {
        // Sum the rotations of the model and the camera to ensure it
        // is rotated to the correct position relative to the model's
        // rotation
        Vector3 combinedRotation = FollowTargetRotation +
        RelativeCameraRotation;

        // Calculate the rotation matrix for the camera
        Matrix rotation = Matrix.CreateFromYawPitchRoll(
            combinedRotation.Y, combinedRotation.X, combinedRotation.Z);

        // Calculate the position the camera would be without the spring
        // value, using the rotation matrix and target position
        Vector3 desiredPosition = FollowTargetPosition +
            Vector3.Transform(PositionOffset, rotation);

        // Interpolate between the current position and desired position
        Position = Vector3.Lerp(Position, desiredPosition, Springiness);

        // Calculate the new target using the rotation matrix
        Target = FollowTargetPosition +  Vector3.Transform(TargetOffset,
        rotation);

        // Obtain the up vector from the matrix
        Vector3 up = Vector3.Transform(Vector3.Up, rotation);

        // Recalculate the view matrix
        View = Matrix.CreateLookAt(Position, Target, up);
    }
}
```

Example—spaceship simulator

Let's use the concepts and classes learned and created so far to create a simple game in which the player flies our spaceship around using the keyboard. You'll notice that the example uses the `ChaseCamera` to follow the spaceship and uses two models to represent the ground and spaceship.

1. We'll start by instantiating these values in the `LoadContent()` method:

```
models.Add(new CModel(Content.Load<Model>("ship"),
    new Vector3(0, 400, 0), Vector3.Zero, new Vector3(0.4f),
    GraphicsDevice));

models.Add(new CModel(Content.Load<Model>("ground"),
    Vector3.Zero, Vector3.Zero, Vector3.One, GraphicsDevice));

camera = new ChaseCamera(new Vector3(0, 400, 1500),
        new Vector3(0, 200, 0),
        new Vector3(0, 0, 0), GraphicsDevice);
```

2. Next, we will create a new function that updates the position and rotation of our model based on keyboard input, which is called by the `Update()` function:

```
// Called when the game should update itself
protected override void Update(GameTime gameTime)
{
    updateModel(gameTime);
    updateCamera(gameTime);

    base.Update(gameTime);
}

void updateModel(GameTime gameTime)
{
    KeyboardState keyState = Keyboard.GetState();

    Vector3 rotChange = new Vector3(0, 0, 0);

    // Determine on which axes the ship should be rotated on, if any
    if (keyState.IsKeyDown(Keys.W))
        rotChange += new Vector3(1, 0, 0);
    if (keyState.IsKeyDown(Keys.S))
        rotChange += new Vector3(-1, 0, 0);
    if (keyState.IsKeyDown(Keys.A))
        rotChange += new Vector3(0, 1, 0);
    if (keyState.IsKeyDown(Keys.D))
        rotChange += new Vector3(0, -1, 0);

    models[0].Rotation += rotChange * .025f;
```

```
    // If space isn't down, the ship shouldn't move
    if (!keyState.IsKeyDown(Keys.Space))
        return;

    // Determine what direction to move in
    Matrix rotation = Matrix.CreateFromYawPitchRoll(
        models[0].Rotation.Y, models[0].Rotation.X,
        models[0].Rotation.Z);

    // Move in the direction dictated by our rotation matrix
    models[0].Position += Vector3.Transform(Vector3.Forward,
        rotation) * (float)gameTime.ElapsedGameTime.TotalMilliseconds *
        4;
}
```

3. We can now greatly simplify the `updateCamera()` function:

```
void updateCamera(GameTime gameTime)
{
    // Move the camera to the new model's position and orientation
    ((ChaseCamera)camera).Move(models[0].Position,
        models[0].Rotation);

    // Update the camera
    camera.Update();
}
```

4. And with that, we're finished! Run your game one last time and you should be able to fly the ship around with *W, S, A, D,* and the *Space bar*:

XNA Graphics Profiles

In an effort to allow developers to easily maintain compatibility with a wide range of devices, XNA provides two "graphics profiles." A **graphics profile** is a set of features that are guaranteed to work on a certain machine, as long as the machine meets all of the requirements of that graphics profile. The two profiles XNA provides are "Reach" and "HiDef." Games developed with the Reach profile will work on a very large range of devices, but are limited in which graphics features they can use. Games developed with the HiDef profile will be able to use a large range of graphics features but they will only work on a much more limited range of devices. The Xbox 360 supports the HiDef profile.

In order to implement many of the examples in this book, you will need to be developing under the Hidef profile. Some examples may work under the Reach profile but this book assumes you are working on a computer supporting HiDef. If you encounter errors while trying to build or run an example, you should first ensure that the game is set to run under the HiDef profile. To do this, right click on your game's project in the solution explorer in Visual Studio (labelled "MyGame" if you have been following along) and click "Properties." Under the "XNA Game Studio" tab, select "Use HiDef to access the complete API (including features unavailable for Windows Phone." Rebuild the game and run it and any errors relating to the graphics profile will be fixed. More information can be found at `http://msdn.microsoft.com/en-us/library/ff604995.aspx`.

Summary

Now that you have completed this chapter, you have an understanding of the fundamentals of 3D graphics. You know how to create a new game project with Visual Studio, how to add content to its content project, and how to remove content. You also have a basic understanding of the content pipeline and how to interact with it through code and the `ContentManager`. You have also created a number of useful classes that will be reused later, including the `CModel` and `Camera` classes, and all of the derived camera classes. Finally, you also have a way to determine which objects intersect others or which are onscreen.

In the coming chapters, we will learn how to add new special effects to our games. We will start with "Effects" (which were mentioned earlier) and HLSL to implement some lighting and texturing effects.

2
Introduction to HLSL

Most of the special effects that we will be discussing in this book will rely in some way on what are called shaders. **Shaders** are pieces of code that are run on the graphics card in parts of what are called the **programmable pipeline**. These pieces of code are written in what is called **HLSL** or the **High Level Shader Language**. Shaders are loaded and executed on the graphics card, which allows them to run very quickly and in parallel, directly with the vertices, textures, and so on that have been loaded into the graphics card's memory.

XNA concerns itself with two types of shaders—the **vertex shader** and the **pixel shader**. The vertex shader and pixel shader are contained in the same code file called an `Effect`. The vertex shader is responsible for transforming geometry from object space into screen space, usually using the world, view, and projection matrices (we learned about this in the last chapter). The pixel shader's job is to calculate the color of every pixel onscreen. It is giving information about the geometry visible at whatever point onscreen it is being run for and takes into account lighting, texturing, and so on.

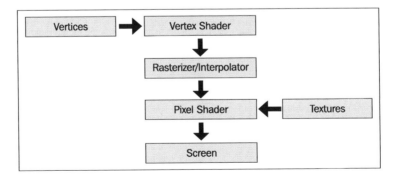

We will spend this chapter learning how to build effects and shaders, and then use that information to write some simple effects that will become the foundation of our work in later chapters.

Getting started

For your convenience, I've provided the starting code for this chapter here. It is comparable to the code we had arrived at the end of the last chapter, but the camera has been switched back to a free camera:

```csharp
public class Game1 : Microsoft.Xna.Framework.Game
{
  GraphicsDeviceManager graphics;
  SpriteBatch spriteBatch;

  List<CModel> models = new List<CModel>();
  Camera camera;

  MouseState lastMouseState;

  public Game1()
  {
     graphics = new GraphicsDeviceManager(this);
     Content.RootDirectory = "Content";

     graphics.PreferredBackBufferWidth = 1280;
     graphics.PreferredBackBufferHeight = 800;
  }

  // Called when the game should load its content
  protected override void LoadContent()
  {
    spriteBatch = new SpriteBatch(GraphicsDevice);

    models.Add(new CModel(Content.Load<Model>("ship"),
        new Vector3(0, 400, 0), Vector3.Zero, new Vector3(1f),
        GraphicsDevice));

    models.Add(new CModel(Content.Load<Model>("ground"), Vector3.Zero,
        Vector3.Zero, Vector3.One, GraphicsDevice));

     camera = new FreeCamera(new Vector3(1000, 500, -2000),
        MathHelper.ToRadians(153), // Turned around 153 degrees
        MathHelper.ToRadians(5), // Pitched up 13 degrees
        GraphicsDevice);
     lastMouseState = Mouse.GetState();
  }

  // Called when the game should update itself
  protected override void Update(GameTime gameTime)
```

```
{
  updateCamera(gameTime);

  base.Update(gameTime);
}

void updateCamera(GameTime gameTime)
{
  // Get the new keyboard and mouse state
  MouseState mouseState = Mouse.GetState();
  KeyboardState keyState = Keyboard.GetState();

  // Determine how much the camera should turn
  float deltaX = (float)lastMouseState.X - (float)mouseState.X;
  float deltaY = (float)lastMouseState.Y - (float)mouseState.Y;

  // Rotate the camera
  ((FreeCamera)camera).Rotate(deltaX * .005f, deltaY * .005f);

  Vector3 translation = Vector3.Zero;

  // Determine in which direction to move the camera
  if (keyState.IsKeyDown(Keys.W)) translation += Vector3.Forward;
  if (keyState.IsKeyDown(Keys.S)) translation += Vector3.Backward;
  if (keyState.IsKeyDown(Keys.A)) translation += Vector3.Left;
  if (keyState.IsKeyDown(Keys.D)) translation += Vector3.Right;

  // Move 3 units per millisecond, independent of frame rate
  translation *= 4 *
  (float)gameTime.ElapsedGameTime.TotalMilliseconds;

  // Move the camera
  ((FreeCamera)camera).Move(translation);

  // Update the camera
  camera.Update();

  // Update the mouse state
  lastMouseState = mouseState;
}

// Called when the game should draw itself
protected override void Draw(GameTime gameTime)
{
```

```
GraphicsDevice.Clear(Color.CornflowerBlue);

foreach (CModel model in models)
if (camera.BoundingVolumeIsInView(model.BoundingSphere))
    model.Draw(camera.View, camera.Projection,
    ((FreeCamera)camera).Position);

base.Draw(gameTime);
    }
}
```

Assigning a shader to a model

In order to draw a model with XNA, it needs to have an instance of the `Effect` class assigned to it. Recall from the first chapter that each `ModelMeshPart` in a `Model` has its own `Effect`. This is because each `ModelMeshPart` may need to have a different appearance, as one `ModelMeshPart` may, for example, make up armor on a soldier while another may make up the head. If the two used the same effect (shader), then we could end up with a very shiny head or a very dull piece of armor. Instead, XNA provides us the option to give every `ModelMeshPart` a unique effect.

As you may remember from the first chapter, by default, each `ModelMeshPart` is loaded by the standard content pipeline model processor with an instance of the `BasicEffect` class assigned to it. In order to draw our models with our own effects, we need to replace the `BasicEffect` of every `ModelMeshPart` with our own effect loaded from the content pipeline. For now, we won't worry about the fact that each `ModelMeshPart` can have its own effect; we'll just be assigning one effect to an entire model. Later, however, we will add more functionality to allow different effects on each part of a model.

However, before we start replacing the instances of `BasicEffect` assigned to our models, we need to extract some useful information from them, such as which texture and color to use for each `ModelMeshPart`. We will store this information in a new class that each `ModelMeshPart` will keep a reference to using its `Tag` properties:

```
public class MeshTag
{
  public Vector3 Color;
  public Texture2D Texture;
  public float SpecularPower;
  public Effect CachedEffect = null;

  public MeshTag(Vector3 Color, Texture2D Texture,
  float SpecularPower)
```

```
    {
        this.Color = Color;
        this.Texture = Texture;
        this.SpecularPower = SpecularPower;
    }
}
```

This information will be extracted using a new function in the `CModel` class:

```
private void generateTags()
{
    foreach (ModelMesh mesh in Model.Meshes)
        foreach (ModelMeshPart part in mesh.MeshParts)
            if (part.Effect is BasicEffect)
            {
                BasicEffect effect = (BasicEffect)part.Effect;
                MeshTag tag = new MeshTag(effect.DiffuseColor, effect.Texture,
                    effect.SpecularPower);
                part.Tag = tag;
            }
}
```

This function will be called along with `buildBoundingSphere()` in the constructor:

```
    . . .

    buildBoundingSphere();
    generateTags();

    . . .
```

Notice that the `MeshTag` class has a `CachedEffect` variable that is not currently used. We will use this value as a location to store a reference to an effect that we want to be able to restore to the `ModelMeshPart` on demand. This is useful when we want to draw a model using a different effect temporarily without having to completely reload the model's effects afterwards. The functions that will allow us to do this are as shown:

```
// Store references to all of the model's current effects
public void CacheEffects()
{
    foreach (ModelMesh mesh in Model.Meshes)
        foreach (ModelMeshPart part in mesh.MeshParts)
            ((MeshTag)part.Tag).CachedEffect = part.Effect;
}

// Restore the effects referenced by the model's cache
```

```
public void RestoreEffects()
{
  foreach (ModelMesh mesh in Model.Meshes)
    foreach (ModelMeshPart part in mesh.MeshParts)
      if (((MeshTag)part.Tag).CachedEffect != null)
        part.Effect = ((MeshTag)part.Tag).CachedEffect;
}
```

We are now ready to start assigning effects to our models. We will look at this in more detail in a moment, but it is worth noting that every Effect has a dictionary of **effect parameters**. These are variables that the Effect takes into account when performing its calculations—the world, view, and projection matrices, or colors and textures, for example. We modify a number of these parameters when assigning a new effect, so that each texture of ModelMeshPart can be informed of its specific properties (which we extracted earlier from BasicEffect):

```
public void SetModelEffect(Effect effect, bool CopyEffect)
{
  foreach(ModelMesh mesh in Model.Meshes)
    foreach (ModelMeshPart part in mesh.MeshParts)
    {
      Effect toSet = effect;

      // Copy the effect if necessary
      if (CopyEffect)
        toSet = effect.Clone();

      MeshTag tag = ((MeshTag)part.Tag);

      // If this ModelMeshPart has a texture, set it to the effect
      if (tag.Texture != null)
      {
        setEffectParameter(toSet, "BasicTexture", tag.Texture);
        setEffectParameter(toSet, "TextureEnabled", true);

      }
      else
        setEffectParameter(toSet, "TextureEnabled", false);

      // Set our remaining parameters to the effect
      setEffectParameter(toSet, "DiffuseColor", tag.Color);
      setEffectParameter(toSet, "SpecularPower", tag.SpecularPower);

      part.Effect = toSet;
    }
}

// Sets the specified effect parameter to the given effect, if it
// has that parameter
```

```
void setEffectParameter(Effect effect, string paramName, object val)
{
  if (effect.Parameters[paramName] == null)
    return;

  if (val is Vector3)
    effect.Parameters[paramName].SetValue((Vector3)val);
  else if (val is bool)
    effect.Parameters[paramName].SetValue((bool)val);
  else if (val is Matrix)
    effect.Parameters[paramName].SetValue((Matrix)val);
  else if (val is Texture2D)
    effect.Parameters[paramName].SetValue((Texture2D)val);
}
```

The `CopyEffect` parameter, an option that this function has, is very important. If we specify `false`—telling the `CModel` not to copy the effect per `ModelMeshPart`—any changes made to the effect will be reflected any other time the effect is used. This is a problem if we want each `ModelMeshPart` to have a different texture, or if we want to use the same effect on multiple models. Instead, we can specify `true` to have the `CModel` copy the effect for each mesh part so that they can set their own effect parameters:

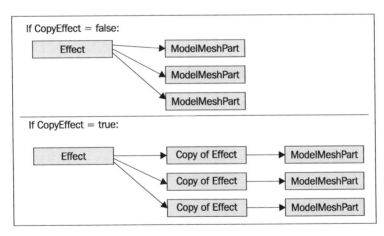

Finally, we need to update the `Draw()` function to handle Effects other than `BasicEffect`:

```
public void Draw(Matrix View, Matrix Projection, Vector3
CameraPosition)
{
  // Calculate the base transformation by combining
  // translation, rotation, and scaling
```

```
Matrix baseWorld = Matrix.CreateScale(Scale)
  * Matrix.CreateFromYawPitchRoll(Rotation.Y, Rotation.X,
    Rotation.Z)
  * Matrix.CreateTranslation(Position);

foreach (ModelMesh mesh in Model.Meshes)
{
    Matrix localWorld = modelTransforms[mesh.ParentBone.Index] *
    baseWorld;

    foreach (ModelMeshPart meshPart in mesh.MeshParts)
    {
      Effect effect = meshPart.Effect;

      if (effect is BasicEffect)
      {
        ((BasicEffect)effect).World = localWorld;
        ((BasicEffect)effect).View = View;
        ((BasicEffect)effect).Projection = Projection;
        ((BasicEffect)effect).EnableDefaultLighting();
      }
      else
      {
        setEffectParameter(effect, "World", localWorld);
        setEffectParameter(effect, "View", View);
        setEffectParameter(effect, "Projection", Projection);
        setEffectParameter(effect, "CameraPosition", CameraPosition);
      }
    }

  mesh.Draw();
  }
}
```

Creating a simple effect

We will create our first effect now, and assign it to our models so that we can see the result. To begin, right-click on the content project, choose **Add New Item**, and select **Effect File**. Call it something like `SimpleEffect.fx`:

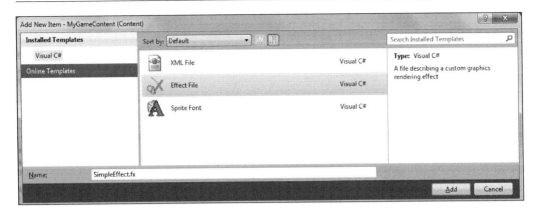

The code for the new file is as follows. Don't worry, we'll go through each piece in a moment:

```
float4x4 World;
float4x4 View;
float4x4 Projection;

struct VertexShaderInput
{
  float4 Position : POSITION0;
};

struct VertexShaderOutput
{
  float4 Position : POSITION0;
};

VertexShaderOutput VertexShaderFunction(VertexShaderInput input)
{
  VertexShaderOutput output;

  float4 worldPosition = mul(input.Position, World);
  float4x4 viewProjection = mul(View, Projection);

  output.Position = mul(worldPosition, viewProjection);

  return output;
}
```

```
float4 PixelShaderFunction(VertexShaderOutput input) : COLOR0
{
  return float4(.5, .5, .5, 1);
}

technique Technique1
{
  pass Pass1
  {
     VertexShader = compile vs_1_1 VertexShaderFunction();
     PixelShader = compile ps_2_0 PixelShaderFunction();
  }
}
```

To assign this effect to the models in our scene, we need to first load it in the game's LoadContent() function, then use the SetModelEffect() function to assign the effect to each model. Add the following to the end of the LoadContent function:

```
Effect simpleEffect = Content.Load<Effect>("SimpleEffect");

models[0].SetModelEffect(simpleEffect, true);
models[1].SetModelEffect(simpleEffect, true);
```

If you were to run the game now, you would notice that the models appear both flat and gray. This is the correct behavior, as the effect doesn't have the code necessary to do anything else at the moment. After we break down each piece of the shader, we will add some more exciting behavior:

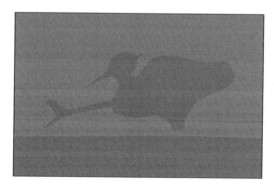

Let's begin at the top. The first three lines in this effect are its effect paremeters. These three should be familiar to you—they are the world, view, and projection matrices (in HLSL, float4x4 is the equivalent of XNA's Matrix class). There are many types of effect parameters and we will see more later.

```
float4x4 World;
float4x4 View;
float4x4 Projection;
```

The next few lines are where we define the structures used in the shaders. In this case, the two structs are `VertexShaderInput` and `VertexShaderOutput`. As you might guess, these two structs are used to send input into the vertex shader and retrieve the output from it. The data in the `VertexShaderOutput` struct is then interpolated between vertices and sent to the pixel shader. This way, when we access the `Position` value in the pixel shader for a pixel that sits between two vertices, we will get the actual position of that location instead of the position of one of the two vertices. In this case, the input and output are very simple: just the position of the vertex before and after it has been transformed using the world, view, and projection matrices:

```
struct VertexShaderInput
{
  float4 Position : POSITION0;
};


struct VertexShaderOutput
{
  float4 Position : POSITION0;
};
```

You may note that the members of these structs are a little different from the properties of a class in C#—in that they must also include what are called **semantics**. Microsoft's definition for shader semantics is as follows (http://msdn.microsoft.com/en-us/library/bb509647%28VS.85%29.aspx):

> *A semantic is a string attached to a shader input or output that conveys information about the intended use of a parameter.*

Basically, we need to specify what we intend to do with each member of our structs so that the graphics card can correctly map the vertex shader's outputs with the pixel shader's inputs. For example, in the previous code, we use the `POSITION0` semantics to tell the graphics card that this value is the one that holds the position at which to draw the vertex.

The next few lines are the vertex shader itself. Basically, we are just multiplying the input (object space or untransformed) vertex position by the world, view, and projection matrices (the `mul` function is part of HLSL and is used to multiply matrices and vertices) and returning that value in a new instance of the `VertexShaderOutput` struct:

```
VertexShaderOutput VertexShaderFunction(VertexShaderInput input)
{
  VertexShaderOutput output;

  float4 worldPosition = mul(input.Position, World);
```

```
    float4x4 viewProjection = mul(View, Projection);

    output.Position = mul(worldPosition, viewProjection);

    return output;
}
```

The next bit of code makes up the pixel shader. It accepts a `VertexShaderOutput` struct as its input (which is passed from the vertex shader), and returns a `float4` — equivelent to XNA's `Vector4` class, in that it is basically a set of four floating point (decimal) numbers. We use the `COLOR0` semantic for our return value to let the pipeline know that this function is returning the final pixel color. In this case, we are using those numbers to represent the red, green, blue, and transparency values respectively of the pixel that we are shading. In this extremely simple pixel shader, we are just returning the color gray (`.5`, `.5`, `.5`), so any pixel covered by the model we are drawing will be gray (like in the previous screenshot).

```
float4 PixelShaderFunction(VertexShaderOutput input) : COLOR0
{
    return float4(.5, .5, .5, 1);
}
```

The last part of the shader is the shader definition. Here, we tell the graphics card which vertex and pixel shader versions to use (every graphics card supports a different set, but in this case we are using vertex shader 1.1 and pixel shader 2.0) and which functions in our code make up the vertex and pixel shaders:

```
technique Technique1
{
  pass Pass1
  {
      VertexShader = compile vs_1_1 VertexShaderFunction();
      PixelShader = compile ps_2_0 PixelShaderFunction();
  }
}
```

Texture mapping

Let's now improve our shader by allowing it to render the textures each `ModelMeshPart` has assigned. As you may recall, the `SetModelEffect` function in the `CModel` class attempts to set the texture of each `ModelMeshPart` to its respective effect. However, it attempts to do so only if it finds the `BasicTexture` parameter on the effect. Let's add this parameter to our effect now (under the world, view, and projection properties):

```
texture BasicTexture;
```

We need one more parameter in order to draw textures on our models, and that is an instance of a `sampler`. The `sampler` is used by HLSL to retrieve the color of the pixel at a given position in a texture—which will be useful later on—in our pixel shader where we will need to retrieve the pixel from the texture corresponding the point on the model we are shading:

```
sampler BasicTextureSampler = sampler_state {
    texture = <BasicTexture>;
};
```

A third effect parameter will allow us to turn texturing on and off:

```
bool TextureEnabled = false;
```

Every model that has a texture should also have what are called texture coordinates. The **texture coordinates** are basically two-dimensional coordinates called **UV coordinates** that range from (0, 0) to (1, 1) and that are assigned to every vertex in the model. These coordinates correspond to the point on the texture that should be drawn onto that vertex. A UV coordinate of (0, 0) corresponds to the top-left of the texture and (1, 1) corresponds to the bottom-right. The texture coordinates allow us to wrap two-dimensional textures onto the three-dimensional surfaces of our models. We need to include the texture coordinates in the input and output of the vertex shader, and add the code to pass the UV coordinates through the vertex shader to the pixel shader:

```
struct VertexShaderInput
{
    float4 Position : POSITION0;
    float2 UV : TEXCOORD0;
};

struct VertexShaderOutput
{
    float4 Position : POSITION0;
    float2 UV : TEXCOORD0;
};

VertexShaderOutput VertexShaderFunction(VertexShaderInput input)
{
    VertexShaderOutput output;

    float4 worldPosition = mul(input.Position, World);
    float4x4 viewProjection = mul(View, Projection);

    output.Position = mul(worldPosition, viewProjection);

    output.UV = input.UV;

    return output;
}
```

Finally, we can use the texture sampler, the texture coordinates (also called UV coordinates), and HLSL's `tex2D` function to retrieve the texture color corresponding to the pixel we are drawing on the model:

```
float4 PixelShaderFunction(VertexShaderOutput input) : COLOR0
{
  float3 output = float3(1, 1, 1);

  if (TextureEnabled)
    output *= tex2D(BasicTextureSampler, input.UV);

  return float4(output, 1);
}
```

If you run the game now, you will see that the textures are properly drawn onto the models:

Texture sampling

The problem with texture sampling is that we are rarely able to simply copy each pixel from a texture directly onto the screen because our models bend and distort the texture due to their shape. Textures are distorted further by the transformations we apply to our models—rotation and other transformations. This means that we almost always have to calculate the approximate position in a texture to sample from and return that value, which is what HLSL's `sampler2D` does for us. There are a number of considerations to make when sampling.

How we sample from our textures can have a big impact on both our game's appearance and performance. More advanced sampling (or filtering) algorithms look better but slow down the game. **Mip mapping** refers to the use of multiple sizes of the same texture. These multiple sizes are calculated before the game is run and stored in the same texture, and the graphics card will swap them out on the fly, using a smaller version of the texture for objects in the distance, and so on. Finally, the *address mode* that we use when sampling will affect how the graphics card handles UV coordinates outside the (0, 1) range. For example, if the address mode is set to "clamp", the UV coordinates will be clamped to (0, 1). If the address mode is set to "wrap," the coordinates will be wrapped through the texture repeatedly. This can be used to create a tiling effect on terrain, for example.

For now, because we are drawing so few models, we will use **anisotropic filtering**. We will also enable mip mapping and set the address mode to "wrap".

```
sampler BasicTextureSampler = sampler_state {
    texture = <BasicTexture>;
    MinFilter = Anisotropic; // Minification Filter
    MagFilter = Anisotropic; // Magnification Filter
    MipFilter = Linear; // Mip-mapping
    AddressU = Wrap; // Address Mode for U Coordinates
    AddressV = Wrap; // Address Mode for V Coordinates
};
```

This will give our models a nice, smooth appearance in the foreground and a uniform appearance in the background:

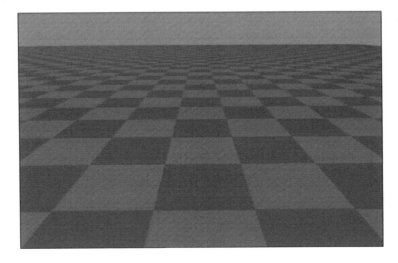

Diffuse colors

Looking at the screenshot that appears immediately before the *Texture sampling* section, there is a problem with our render: some parts of the model are completely white. This is because this particular model does not have textures assigned to those pieces. Right now, if we don't have a texture assigned, our effect simply defaults to white. However, this model also specifies what are called **diffuse colors**. These are basic color values assigned to each `ModelMeshPart`. In this case, drawing the diffuse colors will fix our problem. We are already loading the diffuse colors into the `MeshTag` class, so all we need to do is add a parameter for them to our effect:

```
float3 DiffuseColor = float3(1, 1, 1);
```

Now we can make a small change to our pixel shader to use the diffuse color values instead of white:

```
float3 output = DiffuseColor;
```

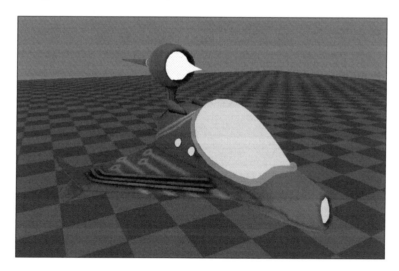

Ambient lighting

Our model is now textured correctly and is using the correct diffuse color values, but it still looks flat and uninteresting. With the groundwork out of the way, we can start recreating some of the lighting effects provided by the `BasicEffect` shader. Let's start with ambient lighting: **Ambient lighting** is an attempt at simulating all the light that bounces off of other objects, the ground, and so on, which would be found in the real world. If you look at an object that doesn't have light shining directly onto it, you can still see it because light has bounced off of other objects nearby and lit it somewhat. As we can't possibly simulate all the bounced rays of light (technically, we can with a technique called *ray tracing*, but this is very slow), we instead simplify it into a constant color value. To add an ambient light value, we simply add another effect parameter:

```
float3 AmbientLightColor = float3(.1, .1, .1);
```

Now, we once again need only a small modification to the pixel shader:

```
float3 output = DiffuseColor + AmbientColor;
```

This will produce the following output (if you're following along with the code files, I've changed the model to a teapot at this point, as it will demonstrate lighting better due to its shape). The object should now look darker, as this light is mainly meant to fill in darker areas as though light were being bounced onto the object from its surroundings.

Lambertian directional lighting

Our next lighting type, **directional lighting**, is meant to provide some definition to our objects. The formula used for this lighting type is called **Lambertian lighting**, and is very simple:

kdiff = max(l • n, 0)

This equation simply means that the lighting amount on a given face is the dot product of the light vector and the face's normal. The dot product is defined as:

X • Y = |X| |Y| cos θ

In the previous equation, θ is the angle between the two vectors. $|X|$ means the length of vector X. Because our vectors are normalized (their length is 1), we can disregard those calculations. The result is that the dot product is simply $cos\ \theta$: 1 if the two vectors are parallel, and 0 if they are perpendicular. This is perfect for lighting, as the dot product of the normal and light direction will return 1 if the light is shining directly onto the surface (parallel to the normal vector), and 0 if it is perpendicular to the surface. In the *Lambertian lighting* equation, we clamp the light value to 0 to avoid negative light values.

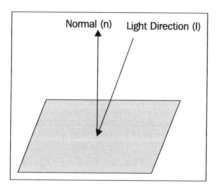

To perform this lighting calculation, we need to retrieve the normals in the vertex shader so that they can be passed to the pixel shader where the calculation is done. We first need to update our vertex shader's input and output structs. (Note that the output uses the `TEXCOORD1` semantic to store the normals. There are numerous texture coordinate channels, and they can be used to store data that is not strictly texture coordinates or of type `float2`.):

```
struct VertexShaderInput
{
  float4 Position : POSITION0;
  float2 UV : TEXCOORD0;
  float3 Normal : NORMAL0;
};

struct VertexShaderOutput
{
  float4 Position : POSITION0;
  float2 UV : TEXCOORD0;
  float3 Normal : TEXCOORD1;
};
```

We next need to update the vertex shader to transform the normals passed in (which are in object space) with the world matrix to move them into world space. The following line does just this, and should be inserted before the `VertexShaderOutput` is returned from the vertex shader. Note that the value is "normalized" with the `normalize()` function. This resizes the normal vector to length 1 as it may have been scaled by the world matrix, which would cause the lighting to be incorrect later on. As discussed earlier, keeping our vectors at length 1 keeps dot products simple.

```
output.Normal = mul(input.Normal, World);
```

We also need to add a parameter at the beginning of the effect for the light direction. While we're at it, we will also add a parameter for the light color:

```
float3 LightDirection = float3(1, 1, 1);
float3 LightColor = float3(0.9, 0.9, 0.9);
```

Finally, we can update the pixel shader to perform the lighting calculation. Note that once again we use the normalize function, this time to ensure that the user-given light vector's components fall within the -1 to 1 range. The dot product of the vertex's normal and the light direction is multiplied by the light color and added to the total amount of light. Note that the `saturate()` function clamps the bottom end of a number to 0 to avoid negative light amounts:

```
float4 PixelShaderFunction(VertexShaderOutput input) : COLOR0
{
  // Start with diffuse color
  float3 color = DiffuseColor;

  // Texture if necessary
  if (TextureEnabled)
     color *= tex2D(BasicTextureSampler, input.UV);

  // Start with ambient lighting
  float3 lighting = AmbientColor;

  float3 lightDir = normalize(LightDirection);
  float3 normal = normalize(input.Normal);

  // Add lambertian lighting
  lighting += saturate(dot(lightDir, normal)) * LightColor;

  // Calculate final color
  float3 output = saturate(lighting) * color;

   return float4(output, 1);
}
```

This produces the effect of a light falling diagonally across the model, and highlights its edges well:

Phong specular highlights

Our object is now looking very defined, but it is still missing one thing: specular highlights. **Specular highlights** is the formal term for the "shininess" you see when looking at the reflection of a light source on an object's surface. Think of the highlights like you are looking at a light bulb through a mirror—you can clearly see the light source. Now, fog the mirror. You can't see the light source, but you can see the circular gradiant effect where the light source would appear on a shinier surface. It should be no surprise, then, that the formula for calculating specular highlights (what is called the *phong shading model*) is as follows:

kspec = max(r • v, 0)n

Translate this to a mirror: *r* is the ray of the light bouncing off from the light source of the mirror (a mirror of our last equation's *l*), and *v* is the view direction. Given the behavior of the last equation and the dot product, it would make sense that the closer *v*, or the direction your eye is facing is to the reflected light vector, the brighter the specular highlight would appear. If you were to move your eye far enough across the mirror, you would lose sight of the light entirely. In that case, there would be no specular highlight as you no longer have light reflecting across the mirror into your eye.

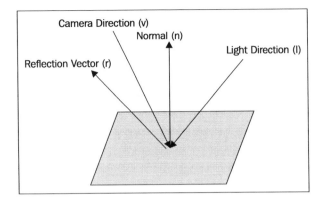

The previous equation also includes an *n* exponent. This, however, unlike the last equation, is not meant to be the normal of the polygon, but rather the "shininess" of the object. As the result of the dot product is between 0 and 1, the higher the *n* exponent value, the closer to 0 the result of raising it to an exponent will be, and thus the duller and smaller the highlight will appear. In order to implement this, we will need three more shader parameters:

```
float SpecularPower = 32;
float3 SpecularColor = float3(1, 1, 1);

float3 CameraPosition;
```

The camera position is set automatically by the CModel class, so we can now update the vertex shader to calculate the direction between each vertex and the camera position—the view direction. First, we need to be sure to pass this value out of the vertex shader:

```
struct VertexShaderOutput
{
    float4 Position : POSITION0;
    float2 UV : TEXCOORD0;
    float3 Normal : TEXCOORD1;
    float3 ViewDirection : TEXCOORD2;
};
```

Now we can add a line to the vertex shader to calculate the view direction:

```
output.ViewDirection = worldPosition - CameraPosition;
```

Finally, we can update the pixel shader:

```
float4 PixelShaderFunction(VertexShaderOutput input) : COLOR0
{
    // Start with diffuse color
    float3 color = DiffuseColor;

    // Texture if necessary
    if (TextureEnabled)
        color *= tex2D(BasicTextureSampler, input.UV);

    // Start with ambient lighting
    float3 lighting = AmbientColor;

    float3 lightDir = normalize(LightDirection);
    float3 normal = normalize(input.Normal);

    // Add lambertian lighting
    lighting += saturate(dot(lightDir, normal)) * LightColor;

    float3 refl = reflect(lightDir, normal);
    float3 view = normalize(input.ViewDirection);

    // Add specular highlights
    lighting += pow(saturate(dot(refl, view)), SpecularPower) *
    SpecularColor;

    // Calculate final color
    float3 output = saturate(lighting) * color;

     return float4(output, 1);
}
```

For your convenience, the full shader is reproduced here—the screenshot of the results of our specular highlights, texturing, directional lighting, ambient lighting, and diffuse color:

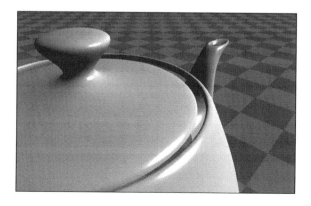

```
float4x4 World;
float4x4 View;
float4x4 Projection;
float3 CameraPosition;

texture BasicTexture;

sampler BasicTextureSampler = sampler_state {
    texture = <BasicTexture>;
    MinFilter = Anisotropic; // Minification Filter
    MagFilter = Anisotropic; // Magnification Filter
    MipFilter = Linear; // Mip-mapping
    AddressU = Wrap; // Address Mode for U Coordinates
    AddressV = Wrap; // Address Mode for V Coordinates
};

bool TextureEnabled = false;

float3 DiffuseColor = float3(1, 1, 1);
float3 AmbientColor = float3(0.1, 0.1, 0.1);
float3 LightDirection = float3(1, 1, 1);
float3 LightColor = float3(0.9, 0.9, 0.9);
float SpecularPower = 32;
float3 SpecularColor = float3(1, 1, 1);

struct VertexShaderInput
{
    float4 Position : POSITION0;
    float2 UV : TEXCOORD0;
    float3 Normal : NORMAL0;
};

struct VertexShaderOutput
{
    float4 Position : POSITION0;
    float2 UV : TEXCOORD0;
    float3 Normal : TEXCOORD1;
    float3 ViewDirection : TEXCOORD2;
};

VertexShaderOutput VertexShaderFunction(VertexShaderInput input)
{
    VertexShaderOutput output;
```

```
        float4 worldPosition = mul(input.Position, World);
        float4x4 viewProjection = mul(View, Projection);

        output.Position = mul(worldPosition, viewProjection);
        output.UV = input.UV;
        output.Normal = mul(input.Normal, World);
        output.ViewDirection = worldPosition - CameraPosition;

        return output;
    }

    float4 PixelShaderFunction(VertexShaderOutput input) : COLOR0
    {
        // Start with diffuse color
        float3 color = DiffuseColor;

        // Texture if necessary
        if (TextureEnabled)
            color *= tex2D(BasicTextureSampler, input.UV);

        // Start with ambient lighting
        float3 lighting = AmbientColor;

        float3 lightDir = normalize(LightDirection);
        float3 normal = normalize(input.Normal);

        // Add lambertian lighting
        lighting += saturate(dot(lightDir, normal)) * LightColor;

        float3 refl = reflect(lightDir, normal);
        float3 view = normalize(input.ViewDirection);

        // Add specular highlights
        lighting += pow(saturate(dot(refl, view)), SpecularPower) *
        SpecularColor;

        // Calculate final color
        float3 output = saturate(lighting) * color;

        return float4(output, 1);
    }

    technique Technique1
    {
```

```
pass Pass1
{
    VertexShader = compile vs_1_1 VertexShaderFunction();
    PixelShader = compile ps_2_0 PixelShaderFunction();
}
}
```

Creating a Material class to store effect parameters

By now we have accumulated a large number of effect parameters in our lighting effect. It would be great if we had an easy way to set and change them from our C# code, so we will add a class called `Material` that does solely this. Each `Model` will have its own material that will store surface properties such as specularity, diffuse color, and so on. This class will then handle setting those properties to an instance of the `Effect` class. As we may have many different types of material, we will also set up a base class:

```
public class Material
{
  public virtual void SetEffectParameters(Effect effect)
  {
  }
}

public class LightingMaterial : Material
{
  public Vector3 AmbientColor { get; set; }
  public Vector3 LightDirection { get; set; }
  public Vector3 LightColor { get; set; }
  public Vector3 SpecularColor { get; set; }

  public LightingMaterial()
  {
     AmbientColor = new Vector3(.1f, .1f, .1f);
     LightDirection = new Vector3(1, 1, 1);
     LightColor = new Vector3(.9f, .9f, .9f);
     SpecularColor = new Vector3(1, 1, 1);
  }

  public override void SetEffectParameters(Effect effect)
  {
```

```
    if (effect.Parameters["AmbientColor"] != null)
        effect.Parameters["AmbientColor"].SetValue(AmbientColor);

    if (effect.Parameters["LightDirection"] != null)
        effect.Parameters["LightDirection"].SetValue(LightDirection);

    if (effect.Parameters["LightColor"] != null)
        effect.Parameters["LightColor"].SetValue(LightColor);

    if (effect.Parameters["SpecularColor"] != null)
        effect.Parameters["SpecularColor"].SetValue(SpecularColor);
    }
}
```

We will now update the `model` class to use the `Material` class. First, we need an instance of the `Material` class:

```
public Material Material { get; set; }
```

We initialize it into a new material in the constructor. As this is the simplest material, no changes will be made to the effect when drawing. This is good as, by default, that effect is a `BasicEffect`, and does not match our parameters.

```
this.Material = new Material();
```

Finally, after the world, view, and projection matrices have been set to the effect in the `Draw()` function, we will call `SetEffectParameters()` on our material:

```
Material.SetEffectParameters(effect);
```

We can finally update the `Game1` class to set the material to the model in the `LoadContent()` method, immediately after setting the effect to the model:

```
Effect simpleEffect = Content.Load<Effect>("LightingEffect");

models[0].SetModelEffect(simpleEffect, true);
models[1].SetModelEffect(simpleEffect, true);

LightingMaterial mat = new LightingMaterial();

models[0].Material = mat;
models[1].Material = mat;
```

So if we now, for example, wanted to light our pot blue with red ambient light, we could set the following options to the `modelMaterial` and they would be automatically reflected onto the shader when the model is drawn:

```
mat.AmbientColor = Color.Red.ToVector3() * .15f;
mat.LightColor = Color.Blue.ToVector3() * .85f;
```

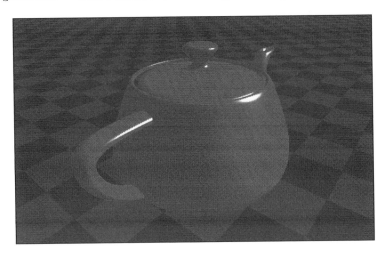

Summary

Now that you've completed this chapter, you've learned the basics of shading—what the programmable pipeline is, what shaders and effects are, and how to write them in HLSL. You saw how to implement a number of lighting types with HLSL, as well as other effects such as diffuse colors and texturing. You upgraded the `CModel` class to support custom shaders and created a `Material` class to manage effect parameters.

If you'd like to know more about HLSL, Microsoft's official documentation is very extensive. It covers all of the built-in functions, filtering, and address modes, and so on, and has several example shaders. It is available at `http://msdn.microsoft.com/en-us/library/bb509638%28VS.85%29.aspx`.

In the next chapter, we will look at more lighting effects and expand our lighting system to support multiple lights. We will look at several ways of doing so and will ultimately create a system that supports an arbitrary number of models and lights while remaining reasonably fast.

3
Advanced Lighting

By the end of the last chapter, we had developed a system to draw a model with custom effects and we had created an effect that rendered a directional light shining onto a model. This is useful if we want a scene with only sunlight, for example, but what if we wanted to light up a specific area? To start with, we'd need a light type that more accurately models real world lights—the "point" light. We will start this chapter by implementing this type of light in HLSL. We will then look at a similar light type—the "spot" light. We will spend the rest of the chapter looking at two ways to draw multiple lights at the same time.

Implementing a point light with HLSL

A **point light** is just a light that shines equally in all directions around itself (like a light bulb) and falls off over a given distance:

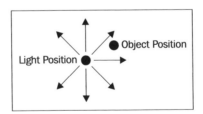

In this case, a point light is simply modeled as a directional light that will slowly fade to darkness over a given distance. To achieve a linear attenuation, we would simply divide the distance between the light and the object by the attenuation distance, invert the result (subtract from 1), and then multiply the lambertian lighting with the result. This would cause an object directly next to the light source to be fully lit, and an object at the maximum attenuation distance to be completely unlit.

However, in practice, we will raise the result of the division to a given power before inverting it to achieve a more exponential falloff:

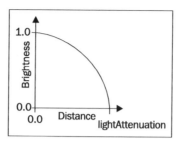

$$K_{att} = 1 - (d / a)^f$$

In the previous equation, K_{att} is the brightness scalar that we will multiply the lighting amount by, d is the distance between the vertex and light source, a is the distance at which the light should stop affecting objects, and f is the falloff exponent that determines the shape of the curve. We can implement this easily with HLSL and a new Material class. The new Material class is similar to the material for a directional light, but specifies a light position rather than a light direction. For the sake of simplicity, the effect we will use will not calculate specular highlights, so the material does not include a "specularity" value. It also includes new values, LightAttenuation and LightFalloff, which specify the distance at which the light is no longer visible and what power to raise the division to.

```
public class PointLightMaterial : Material
{
  public Vector3 AmbientLightColor { get; set; }
  public Vector3 LightPosition { get; set; }
  public Vector3 LightColor { get; set; }
  public float LightAttenuation { get; set; }
    public float LightFalloff { get; set; }

  public PointLightMaterial()
  {
    AmbientLightColor = new Vector3(.15f, .15f, .15f);
    LightPosition = new Vector3(0, 0, 0);
    LightColor = new Vector3(.85f, .85f, .85f);
    LightAttenuation = 5000;
    LightFalloff = 2;
  }

  public override void SetEffectParameters(Effect effect)
  {
    if (effect.Parameters["AmbientLightColor"] != null)
```

```
        effect.Parameters["AmbientLightColor"].SetValue(
          AmbientLightColor);

      if (effect.Parameters["LightPosition"] != null)
          effect.Parameters["LightPosition"].SetValue(LightPosition);

      if (effect.Parameters["LightColor"] != null)
          effect.Parameters["LightColor"].SetValue(LightColor);

      if (effect.Parameters["LightAttenuation"] != null)
          effect.Parameters["LightAttenuation"].SetValue(
            LightAttenuation);

      if (effect.Parameters["LightFalloff"] != null)
          effect.Parameters["LightFalloff"].SetValue(LightFalloff);
    }
}
```

The new effect has parameters to reflect those values:

```
float4x4 World;
float4x4 View;
float4x4 Projection;

float3 AmbientLightColor = float3(.15, .15, .15);
float3 DiffuseColor = float3(.85, .85, .85);
float3 LightPosition = float3(0, 0, 0);
float3 LightColor = float3(1, 1, 1);
float LightAttenuation = 5000;
float LightFalloff = 2;

texture BasicTexture;

sampler BasicTextureSampler = sampler_state {
   texture = <BasicTexture>;
};

bool TextureEnabled = true;
```

The vertex shader output struct now includes a copy of the vertex's world position that will be used to calculate the light falloff (attenuation) and light direction.

```
struct VertexShaderInput
{
  float4 Position : POSITION0;
  float2 UV : TEXCOORD0;
  float3 Normal : NORMAL0;
};
```

```
struct VertexShaderOutput
{
  float4 Position : POSITION0;
  float2 UV : TEXCOORD0;
  float3 Normal : TEXCOORD1;
  float4 WorldPosition : TEXCOORD2;
};

VertexShaderOutput VertexShaderFunction(VertexShaderInput input)
{
  VertexShaderOutput output;

  float4 worldPosition = mul(input.Position, World);
  float4 viewPosition = mul(worldPosition, View);
  output.Position = mul(viewPosition, Projection);

  output.WorldPosition = worldPosition;
  output.UV = input.UV;
  output.Normal = mul(input.Normal, World);

  return output;
}
```

Finally, the pixel shader calculates the light much the same way that the directional light did, but uses a per-vertex light direction rather than a global light direction. It also determines how far along the attenuation value the vertex's position is and darkens it accordingly. The texture, ambient light, and diffuse color are calculated as usual:

```
float4 PixelShaderFunction(VertexShaderOutput input) : COLOR0
{
  float3 diffuseColor = DiffuseColor;

  if (TextureEnabled)
     diffuseColor *= tex2D(BasicTextureSampler, input.UV).rgb;
  float3 totalLight = float3(0, 0, 0);

  totalLight += AmbientLightColor;

  float3 lightDir = normalize(LightPosition - input.WorldPosition);
  float diffuse = saturate(dot(normalize(input.Normal), lightDir));
  float d = distance(LightPosition, input.WorldPosition);
  float att = 1 - pow(clamp(d / LightAttenuation, 0, 1),
   LightFalloff);

  totalLight += diffuse * att * LightColor;

  return float4(diffuseColor * totalLight, 1);
}
```

We can now achieve the above image using the following scene setup from the
Game1 class:

```
models.Add(new CModel(Content.Load<Model>("teapot"),
    new Vector3(0, 60, 0), Vector3.Zero, new Vector3(60),
    GraphicsDevice));

models.Add(new CModel(Content.Load<Model>("ground"),
    Vector3.Zero, Vector3.Zero, Vector3.One, GraphicsDevice));

Effect simpleEffect = Content.Load<Effect>("PointLightEffect");

models[0].SetModelEffect(simpleEffect, true);
models[1].SetModelEffect(simpleEffect, true);

PointLightMaterial mat = new PointLightMaterial();
mat.LightPosition = new Vector3(0, 1500, 1500);
mat.LightAttenuation = 3000;

models[0].Material = mat;
models[1].Material = mat;

camera = new FreeCamera(new Vector3(0, 300, 1600),
    MathHelper.ToRadians(0), // Turned around 153 degrees
    MathHelper.ToRadians(5), // Pitched up 13 degrees
    GraphicsDevice);
```

Implementing a spot light with HLSL

A **spot light** is similar in theory to a point light—in that it fades out after a given distance. However, the fading is not done around the light source, but is based on the angle between the direction of an object and the light source, and the light's actual direction. If the angle is larger than the light's "**cone angle**", we will not light the vertex.

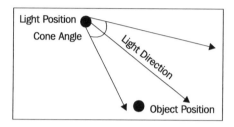

$$K_{att} = (\text{dot}(p - lp, ld) \;/\; \cos(a))^f$$

In the previous equation, Katt is still the scalar that we will multiply our diffuse lighting with, p is the position of the vertex, lp is the position of the light, ld is the direction of the light, a is the cone angle, and f is the falloff exponent. Our new spot light material reflects these values:

```
public class SpotLightMaterial : Material
{
    public Vector3 AmbientLightColor { get; set; }
    public Vector3 LightPosition { get; set; }
    public Vector3 LightColor { get; set; }
    public Vector3 LightDirection { get; set; }
    public float ConeAngle { get; set; }
    public float LightFalloff { get; set; }

    public SpotLightMaterial()
    {
        AmbientLightColor = new Vector3(.15f, .15f, .15f);
        LightPosition = new Vector3(0, 3000, 0);
        LightColor = new Vector3(.85f, .85f, .85f);
        ConeAngle = 30;
        LightDirection = new Vector3(0, -1, 0);
        LightFalloff = 20;
    }

    public override void SetEffectParameters(Effect effect)
    {
```

```
        if (effect.Parameters["AmbientLightColor"] != null)
          effect.Parameters["AmbientLightColor"].SetValue(
            AmbientLightColor);

        if (effect.Parameters["LightPosition"] != null)
          effect.Parameters["LightPosition"].SetValue(LightPosition);

        if (effect.Parameters["LightColor"] != null)
          effect.Parameters["LightColor"].SetValue(LightColor);

        if (effect.Parameters["LightDirection"] != null)
          effect.Parameters["LightDirection"].SetValue(LightDirection);

        if (effect.Parameters["ConeAngle"] != null)
          effect.Parameters["ConeAngle"].SetValue(
            MathHelper.ToRadians(ConeAngle / 2));

        if (effect.Parameters["LightFalloff"] != null)
          effect.Parameters["LightFalloff"].SetValue(LightFalloff);
    }
}
```

Now we can create a new effect that will render a spot light. We will start by copying the point light's effect and making the following changes to the second block of effect parameters:

```
float3 AmbientLightColor = float3(.15, .15, .15);
float3 DiffuseColor = float3(.85, .85, .85);
float3 LightPosition = float3(0, 5000, 0);
float3 LightDirection = float3(0, -1, 0);
float ConeAngle = 90;
float3 LightColor = float3(1, 1, 1);
float LightFalloff = 20;
```

Finally, we can update the pixel shader to perform the lighting calculations:

```
float4 PixelShaderFunction(VertexShaderOutput input) : COLOR0
{
  float3 diffuseColor = DiffuseColor;

  if (TextureEnabled)
    diffuseColor *= tex2D(BasicTextureSampler, input.UV).rgb;

  float3 totalLight = float3(0, 0, 0);
  totalLight += AmbientLightColor;
  float3 lightDir = normalize(LightPosition - input.WorldPosition);
```

```
float diffuse = saturate(dot(normalize(input.Normal), lightDir));

// (dot(p - lp, ld) / cos(a))^f
float d = dot(-lightDir, normalize(LightDirection));
float a = cos(ConeAngle);

float att = 0;

if (a < d)
    att = 1 - pow(clamp(a / d, 0, 1), LightFalloff);

totalLight += diffuse * att * LightColor;

return float4(diffuseColor * totalLight, 1);
}
```

If we were to then set up the material as follows and use our new effect, we would see the following result:

```
SpotLightMaterial mat = new SpotLightMaterial();
mat.LightDirection = new Vector3(0, -1, -1);
mat.LightPosition = new Vector3(0, 3000, 2700);
mat.LightFalloff = 200;
```

Drawing multiple lights

Now that we can draw one light, the natural question to ask is how to draw more than one light. Well this, unfortunately, is not simple. There are a number of approaches—the easiest of which is to simply loop through a certain number of lights in the pixel shader and sum a total lighting value. Let's create a new shader based on the directional light effect that we created in the last chapter to do just that. We'll start by copying that effect, then modifying some of the effect parameters as follows. Notice that instead of a single light direction and color, we instead have an array of three of each, allowing us to draw up to three lights:

```
#define NUMLIGHTS 3

float3 DiffuseColor = float3(1, 1, 1);
float3 AmbientColor = float3(0.1, 0.1, 0.1);
float3 LightDirection[NUMLIGHTS];
float3 LightColor[NUMLIGHTS];
float SpecularPower = 32;
float3 SpecularColor = float3(1, 1, 1);
```

Second, we need to update the pixel shader to do the lighting calculations one time per light:

```
float4 PixelShaderFunction(VertexShaderOutput input) : COLOR0
{
  // Start with diffuse color
  float3 color = DiffuseColor;

  // Texture if necessary
  if (TextureEnabled)
    color *= tex2D(BasicTextureSampler, input.UV);

  // Start with ambient lighting
  float3 lighting = AmbientColor;

  float3 normal = normalize(input.Normal);
  float3 view = normalize(input.ViewDirection);

  // Perform lighting calculations per light
  for (int i = 0; i < NUMLIGHTS; i++)
  {
      float3 lightDir = normalize(LightDirection[i]);

      // Add lambertian lighting
      lighting += saturate(dot(lightDir, normal)) * LightColor[i];
```

```
        float3 refl = reflect(lightDir, normal);

        // Add specular highlights
        lighting += pow(saturate(dot(refl, view)), SpecularPower)
          * SpecularColor;
    }

    // Calculate final color
    float3 output = saturate(lighting) * color;

    return float4(output, 1);
}
```

We now need a new Material class to work with this shader:

```
public class MultiLightingMaterial : Material
{
  public Vector3 AmbientColor { get; set; }
  public Vector3[] LightDirection { get; set; }
  public Vector3[] LightColor { get; set; }
  public Vector3 SpecularColor { get; set; }

  public MultiLightingMaterial()
  {
    AmbientColor = new Vector3(.1f, .1f, .1f);
    LightDirection = new Vector3[3];
    LightColor = new Vector3[] { Vector3.One, Vector3.One,
      Vector3.One };
    SpecularColor = new Vector3(1, 1, 1);
  }

  public override void SetEffectParameters(Effect effect)
  {
    if (effect.Parameters["AmbientColor"] != null)
        effect.Parameters["AmbientColor"].SetValue(AmbientColor);

    if (effect.Parameters["LightDirection"] != null)
        effect.Parameters["LightDirection"].SetValue(LightDirection);

    if (effect.Parameters["LightColor"] != null)
        effect.Parameters["LightColor"].SetValue(LightColor);

    if (effect.Parameters["SpecularColor"] != null)
        effect.Parameters["SpecularColor"].SetValue(SpecularColor);
  }
}
```

If we wanted to implement the three directional light systems found in the `BasicEffect` class, we would now just need to copy the light direction values over to our shader:

```
Effect simpleEffect = Content.Load<Effect>("MultiLightingEffect");

models[0].SetModelEffect(simpleEffect, true);
models[1].SetModelEffect(simpleEffect, true);

MultiLightingMaterial mat = new MultiLightingMaterial();

BasicEffect effect = new BasicEffect(GraphicsDevice);
effect.EnableDefaultLighting();

mat.LightDirection[0] = -effect.DirectionalLight0.Direction;
mat.LightDirection[1] = -effect.DirectionalLight1.Direction;
mat.LightDirection[2] = -effect.DirectionalLight2.Direction;

mat.LightColor = new Vector3[] {
    .new Vector3(0.5f, 0.5f, 0.5f),
    new Vector3(0.5f, 0.5f, 0.5f),
    new Vector3(0.5f, 0.5f, 0.5f) };

models[0].Material = mat;
models[1].Material = mat;
```

Prelighting

This method works, but it limits us to just three lights. In any real game, this number is way too small. We could add more lights to the shader, but we would still be quite limited as we cannot do more because we have a limited number of shader instructions to work with. Our next option would be to concoct a system to draw the scene repeatedly with multiple light sources, and then blend them together. However, this would force us to draw every object in the scene once for every light in the scene—an extremely inefficient approach.

Instead, we will use an approach called **prelighting**. In this approach, we store the information that we need to calculate lighting for a pixel into textures that can then be loaded later on by another shader to do the lighting calculation themselves. This has two benefits: First, we are drawing each object only once. Second, we use spheres to approximate our lights so that we can run a pixel shader on only the pixels a light would affect, limiting the lighting calculations to pixels that are actually affected by a light. Therefore, if a light is small enough or distant enough, we don't need to perform its lighting calculations for every pixel on the screen.

The prelighting process is as follows:

1. Render the scene into two textures, storing the distance of each vertex from the camera and the normal at each vertex.
2. Render the scene into another texture, rendering each (point) light as a sphere, performing lighting calculations in the pixel shader using the values stored in the corresponding pixels of the last step's textures.
3. Render the final scene, multiplying diffuse colors, textures, and so on in the pixel shader by the lighting values stored in the corresponding pixels of the last step's texture.

We will implement prelighting in the next sections. This is a bit of a process, but in the end, you'll be able to draw a large number of lights and models in your scene—well worth the effort as this is a common stumbling block for new game developers. As an example, the following scene was rendered with eight different-colored point lights:

Storing depth and normal values

Recall that we need two pieces of information to calculate simple Lambertian lighting—the position of each vertex and its normals. In a prelighting approach to lighting, we store these two pieces of information into two textures using "multiple render targets". To use multiple render targets, we output multiple values from the pixel shader using multiple COLOR (COLOR0, COLOR1, and so on) semantics. The output from the effect will then be stored into the "render targets" (similar to textures) of our choosing. We will see shortly how this is set up from the XNA side.

We store the distance between each vertex and the camera into one texture and the "depth" texture and each vertex's normal into the second texture. Note that the depth is divided by the far plane distance before storing it into the texture to keep it in the 0 to 1 range:

Similarly, the normals are scaled from the -1 to 1 range to the 0 to 1 range.

The effect that stores the depth and normal values is as follows. Create a new effect in your content project called PPDepthNormal.fx and add the following code:

```
float4x4 World;
float4x4 View;
float4x4 Projection;

struct VertexShaderInput
{
  float4 Position : POSITION0;
  float3 Normal : NORMAL0;
};

struct VertexShaderOutput
{
  float4 Position : POSITION0;
  float2 Depth : TEXCOORD0;
  float3 Normal : TEXCOORD1;
};

VertexShaderOutput VertexShaderFunction(VertexShaderInput input)
{
  VertexShaderOutput output;

  float4x4 viewProjection = mul(View, Projection);
  float4x4 worldViewProjection = mul(World, viewProjection);

  output.Position = mul(input.Position, worldViewProjection);
  output.Normal = mul(input.Normal, World);

  // Position's z and w components correspond to the distance
  // from camera and distance of the far plane respectively
  output.Depth.xy = output.Position.zw;

  return output;
}

// We render to two targets simultaneously, so we can't
// simply return a float4 from the pixel shader
struct PixelShaderOutput
{
  float4 Normal : COLOR0;
  float4 Depth : COLOR1;
};
```

```
PixelShaderOutput PixelShaderFunction(VertexShaderOutput input)
{
  PixelShaderOutput output;

  // Depth is stored as distance from camera / far plane distance
  // to get value between 0 and 1
  output.Depth = input.Depth.x / input.Depth.y;

  // Normal map simply stores X, Y and Z components of normal
  // shifted from (-1 to 1) range to (0 to 1) range
  output.Normal.xyz = (normalize(input.Normal).xyz / 2) + .5;

  // Other components must be initialized to compile
  output.Depth.a = 1;
  output.Normal.a = 1;

  return output;
}

technique Technique1
{
  pass Pass1
  {
    VertexShader = compile vs_1_1 VertexShaderFunction();
    PixelShader = compile ps_2_0 PixelShaderFunction();
  }
}
```

Creating the light map

Once we have our normal and depth values recorded, we can generate the light map. We'll be creating a class in a moment to tie all of the steps together, but first, let's look at the effect that generates light maps. Because the depth and normal values are stored in a texture and we can't pass them from a vertex shader, we need a way to map 3D positions to pixel coordinates in the two textures. For the sake of convenience, we will place the functions that do so in a shared file that will be included in a few of the remaining effects. You'll need to create a new effect file and rename it to PPShared.vsi.

```
float viewportWidth;
float viewportHeight;

// Calculate the 2D screen position of a 3D position
float2 postProjToScreen(float4 position)
```

```
  {
    float2 screenPos = position.xy / position.w;
    return 0.5f * (float2(screenPos.x, -screenPos.y) + 1);
  }


  // Calculate the size of one half of a pixel, to convert
  // between texels and pixels
  float2 halfPixel()
  {
    return 0.5f / float2(viewportWidth, viewportHeight);
  }
```

Now we can create the effect that uses these values to perform the lighting calculations. The effect parameters are fairly self-explanatory—we include texture parameters for the depth and normal textures, world, view, and projection matrices (remember that we are drawing the light as a spherical model), and point light parameters. The vertex shader simply transforms from object space to screen space:

```
float4x4 WorldViewProjection;
float4x4 InvViewProjection;

texture2D DepthTexture;
texture2D NormalTexture;
sampler2D depthSampler = sampler_state
{
  texture = <DepthTexture>;
  minfilter = point;
  magfilter = point;
  mipfilter = point;
};
sampler2D normalSampler = sampler_state
{
  texture = <NormalTexture>;
  minfilter = point;
  magfilter = point;
  mipfilter = point;
};

float3 LightColor;
float3 LightPosition;
float LightAttenuation;

// Include shared functions
#include "PPShared.vsi"
```

```
struct VertexShaderInput
{
  float4 Position : POSITION0;
};

struct VertexShaderOutput
{
  float4 Position : POSITION0;
  float4 LightPosition : TEXCOORD0;
};

VertexShaderOutput VertexShaderFunction(VertexShaderInput input)
{
  VertexShaderOutput output;

  output.Position = mul(input.Position, WorldViewProjection);
  output.LightPosition = output.Position;

  return output;
}
```

The pixel shader is where the magic happens—we sample the depth and normal values from the textures that we rendered earlier and use the depth values to reconstruct our original world space position. We then use that position and its normal to perform the lighting calculations that we saw earlier:

```
float4 PixelShaderFunction(VertexShaderOutput input) : COLOR0
{
  // Find the pixel coordinates of the input position in the depth
  // and normal textures
  float2 texCoord = postProjToScreen(input.LightPosition) +
   halfPixel();

  // Extract the depth for this pixel from the depth map
  float4 depth = tex2D(depthSampler, texCoord);

  // Recreate the position with the UV coordinates and depth value
  float4 position;
  position.x = texCoord.x * 2 - 1;
  position.y = (1 - texCoord.y) * 2 - 1;
  position.z = depth.r;
  position.w = 1.0f;

  // Transform position from screen space to world space
  position = mul(position, InvViewProjection);
```

```
    position.xyz /= position.w;

    // Extract the normal from the normal map and move from
    // 0 to 1 range to -1 to 1 range
    float4 normal = (tex2D(normalSampler, texCoord) - .5) * 2;

    // Perform the lighting calculations for a point light
    float3 lightDirection = normalize(LightPosition - position);
    float lighting = clamp(dot(normal, lightDirection), 0, 1);

    // Attenuate the light to simulate a point light
    float d = distance(LightPosition, position);
    float att = 1 - pow(d / LightAttenuation, 6);

    return float4(LightColor * lighting * att, 1);
}
```

Drawing models with the light map

After we have created the light map, we can sample the values it stores when
drawing our models for the final pass instead of performing the lighting equations.
We will again use the functions in our shared file to sample from the light map. The
rest of the effects are similar to those we have already seen, transforming to screen
space in the vertex shader and performing texture lookups in the pixel shader. At the
end of the pixel shader, we multiply the lighting value sampled from the light map
with the diffuse color to get the final color:

```
float4x4 World;
float4x4 View;
float4x4 Projection;

texture2D BasicTexture;
sampler2D basicTextureSampler = sampler_state
{
    texture = <BasicTexture>;
    addressU = wrap;
    addressV = wrap;
    minfilter = anisotropic;
    magfilter = anisotropic;
    mipfilter = linear;
};
bool TextureEnabled = true;

texture2D LightTexture;
```

```
texture2D LightTexture;
sampler2D lightSampler = sampler_state
{
    texture = <LightTexture>;
    minfilter = point;
    magfilter = point;
    mipfilter = point;
};

float3 AmbientColor = float3(0.15, 0.15, 0.15);
float3 DiffuseColor;

#include "PPShared.vsi"

struct VertexShaderInput
{
    float4 Position : POSITION0;
    float2 UV : TEXCOORD0;
};

struct VertexShaderOutput
{
    float4 Position : POSITION0;
    float2 UV : TEXCOORD0;
    float4 PositionCopy : TEXCOORD1;
};

VertexShaderOutput VertexShaderFunction(VertexShaderInput input)
{
    VertexShaderOutput output;

    float4x4 worldViewProjection = mul(World, mul(View, Projection));

    output.Position = mul(input.Position, worldViewProjection);
    output.PositionCopy = output.Position;

    output.UV = input.UV;

    return output;
}

float4 PixelShaderFunction(VertexShaderOutput input) : COLOR0
{
    // Sample model's texture
```

```
    float3 basicTexture = tex2D(basicTextureSampler, input.UV);

    if (!TextureEnabled)
        basicTexture = float4(1, 1, 1, 1);

    // Extract lighting value from light map
    float2 texCoord = postProjToScreen(input.PositionCopy) +
     halfPixel();
    float3 light = tex2D(lightSampler, texCoord);

    light += AmbientColor;

    return float4(basicTexture * DiffuseColor * light, 1);
}
```

Creating the prelighting renderer

Let's now create a class that manages the effects we created and the rest of the prelighting process. This class, `PrelightingRenderer`, will be responsible for calculating the depth and normal maps, light map, and eventually preparing models to be drawn with the calculated lighting values. The following framework version loads all of the effects and the model that we will need to perform the prelighting process.

The `PrelightingRenderer` also handles the creation of three "surfaces" or "render targets" that we will render the depth, normal, and light maps into. Render targets serve to capture the output of the graphics card and store it in memory, much like a texture. We can then access the data in that texture later, when we are calculating the light map, for example. We can also draw into multiple render targets at the same time using the various color semantics, as we saw earlier in `DepthNormal.fx`.

```
public class PrelightingRenderer
{
    // Normal, depth, and light map render targets
    RenderTarget2D depthTarg;
    RenderTarget2D normalTarg;
    RenderTarget2D lightTarg;

    // Depth/normal effect and light mapping effect
    Effect depthNormalEffect;
    Effect lightingEffect;

    // Point light (sphere) mesh
    Model lightMesh;
```

```
// List of models, lights, and the camera
public List<CModel> Models { get; set; }
public List<PPPointLight> Lights { get; set; }
public Camera Camera { get; set; }

GraphicsDevice graphicsDevice;
int viewWidth = 0, viewHeight = 0;

public PrelightingRenderer(GraphicsDevice GraphicsDevice,
    ContentManager Content)
{
  viewWidth = GraphicsDevice.Viewport.Width;
  viewHeight = GraphicsDevice.Viewport.Height;

  // Create the three render targets
  depthTarg = new RenderTarget2D(GraphicsDevice, viewWidth,
      viewHeight, false, SurfaceFormat.Single, DepthFormat.Depth24);

  normalTarg = new RenderTarget2D(GraphicsDevice, viewWidth,
      viewHeight, false, SurfaceFormat.Color, DepthFormat.Depth24);

  lightTarg = new RenderTarget2D(GraphicsDevice, viewWidth,
      viewHeight, false, SurfaceFormat.Color, DepthFormat.Depth24);

  // Load effects
  depthNormalEffect = Content.Load<Effect>("PPDepthNormal");
  lightingEffect = Content.Load<Effect>("PPLight");

  // Set effect parameters to light mapping effect
  lightingEffect.Parameters["viewportWidth"].SetValue(viewWidth);
  lightingEffect.Parameters["viewportHeight"].SetValue(viewHeight);

  // Load point light mesh and set light mapping effect to it
  lightMesh = Content.Load<Model>("PPLightMesh");
  lightMesh.Meshes[0].MeshParts[0].Effect = lightingEffect;

  this.graphicsDevice = GraphicsDevice;
}

public void Draw()
{
    drawDepthNormalMap();
    drawLightMap();
    prepareMainPass();
}
```

```
    void drawDepthNormalMap()
    {
    }

    void drawLightMap()
    {
    }

    void prepareMainPass()
    {
    }
}
```

Now we can start filling in the three empty functions in the framework of this class. The `drawDepthNormalMap()` function will be responsible for capturing the depth and normal map information from all of the models currently in view. We already wrote the effect that does this, so all we need to do is set our render target and draw the models with the `PPDepthNormal.fx` effect:

```
void drawDepthNormalMap()
{
  // Set the render targets to 'slots' 1 and 2
  graphicsDevice.SetRenderTargets(normalTarg, depthTarg);

  // Clear the render target to 1 (infinite depth)
  graphicsDevice.Clear(Color.White);

  // Draw each model with the PPDepthNormal effect
  foreach (CModel model in Models)
  {
    model.CacheEffects();
    model.SetModelEffect(depthNormalEffect, false);
    model.Draw(Camera.View, Camera.Projection,
        ((FreeCamera)Camera).Position);
    model.RestoreEffects();
  }

  // Un-set the render targets
  graphicsDevice.SetRenderTargets(null);
}
```

The second function takes the depth and normal map data from the first and uses it to perform the lighting calculations for each point light in the scene, approximated as spheres:

```
void drawLightMap()
{
  // Set the depth and normal map info to the effect
  lightingEffect.Parameters["DepthTexture"].SetValue(depthTarg);
  lightingEffect.Parameters["NormalTexture"].SetValue(normalTarg);

  // Calculate the view * projection matrix
  Matrix viewProjection = Camera.View * Camera.Projection;

  // Set the inverse of the view * projection matrix to the effect
  Matrix invViewProjection = Matrix.Invert(viewProjection);
  lightingEffect.Parameters["InvViewProjection"].SetValue(
      invViewProjection);

  // Set the render target to the graphics device
  graphicsDevice.SetRenderTarget(lightTarg);

  // Clear the render target to black (no light)
  graphicsDevice.Clear(Color.Black);

  // Set render states to additive (lights will add their influences)
  graphicsDevice.BlendState = BlendState.Additive;
  graphicsDevice.DepthStencilState = DepthStencilState.None;

  foreach (PPPointLight light in Lights)
  {
    // Set the light's parameters to the effect
    light.SetEffectParameters(lightingEffect);

    // Calculate the world * view * projection matrix and set it to
    // the effect
    Matrix wvp = (Matrix.CreateScale(light.Attenuation)
        * Matrix.CreateTranslation(light.Position)) * viewProjection;

    lightingEffect.Parameters["WorldViewProjection"].SetValue(wvp);

    // Determine the distance between the light and camera
    float dist = Vector3.Distance(((FreeCamera)Camera).Position,
      light.Position);
```

```
        // If the camera is inside the light-sphere, invert the cull mode
        // to draw the inside of the sphere instead of the outside
        if (dist < light.Attenuation)
           graphicsDevice.RasterizerState = RasterizerState.CullClockwise;

        // Draw the point-light-sphere
        lightMesh.Meshes[0].Draw();

        // Revert the cull mode
        graphicsDevice.RasterizerState =
           RasterizerState.CullCounterClockwise;
    }

    // Revert the blending and depth render states
    graphicsDevice.BlendState = BlendState.Opaque;
    graphicsDevice.DepthStencilState = DepthStencilState.Default;

    // Un-set the render target
    graphicsDevice.SetRenderTarget(null);
}
```

The last function, `prepareMainPass()`, attempts to set the light map and viewport width/height to the effect each model is currently using. The models can then sample from the light map to obtain lighting information, as our `PPLight.fx` function does:

```
void prepareMainPass()
{
  foreach (CModel model in Models)
    foreach (ModelMesh mesh in model.Model.Meshes)
      foreach (ModelMeshPart part in mesh.MeshParts)
      {
        // Set the light map and viewport parameters to each model's
           effect
        if (part.Effect.Parameters["LightTexture"] != null)
          part.Effect.Parameters["LightTexture"].SetValue(lightTarg);

        if (part.Effect.Parameters["viewportWidth"] != null)
          part.Effect.Parameters["viewportWidth"].SetValue(viewWidth);

        if (part.Effect.Parameters["viewportHeight"] != null)
          part.Effect.Parameters["viewportHeight"].
            SetValue(viewHeight);
      }
}
```

Using the prelighting renderer

With that, we've finished the prelighting renderer and can now implement it into our game. To begin with, we'll need an instance variable of the `renderer` in the `Game1` class:

```
PrelightingRenderer renderer;
```

Next, we set the scene up as follows in the `LoadContent()` function, using our `PPLight.fx` effect and four point lights:

```
models.Add(new CModel(Content.Load<Model>("teapot"),
    new Vector3(0, 60, 0), Vector3.Zero, new Vector3(60),
    GraphicsDevice));

models.Add(new CModel(Content.Load<Model>("ground"),
    Vector3.Zero, Vector3.Zero, Vector3.One, GraphicsDevice));

Effect effect = Content.Load<Effect>("PPModel");

models[0].SetModelEffect(effect, true);
models[1].SetModelEffect(effect, true);

camera = new FreeCamera(new Vector3(0, 300, 1600),
    MathHelper.ToRadians(0), // Turned around 153 degrees
    MathHelper.ToRadians(5), // Pitched up 13 degrees
    GraphicsDevice);

renderer = new PrelightingRenderer(GraphicsDevice, Content);
renderer.Models = models;
renderer.Camera = camera;
renderer.Lights = new List<PPPointLight>()
{
    new PPPointLight(new Vector3(-1000, 1000, 0), Color.Red * .85f,
        2000),
    new PPPointLight(new Vector3(1000, 1000, 0), Color.Blue * .85f,
        2000),
    new PPPointLight(new Vector3(0, 1000, 1000), Color.Green * .85f,
        2000),
    new PPPointLight(new Vector3(0, 1000, -1000), Color.White * .85f,
        2000)
};
```

Finally, we need to call the `Draw()` function of the `renderer` before drawing our models for the final pass, making sure to clear the graphics card first:

```
protected override void Draw(GameTime gameTime)
{
  renderer.Draw();

  GraphicsDevice.Clear(Color.Black);

  foreach (CModel model in models)
    if (camera.BoundingVolumeIsInView(model.BoundingSphere))
      model.Draw(camera.View, camera.Projection,
        ((FreeCamera)camera).Position);

  base.Draw(gameTime);
}
```

Summary

Having completed this chapter, you've learned how to implement point lights and spot lights in HLSL. You've also learned of the limitations of the programmable pipeline, as far as lighting is concerned, and learned two ways to draw multiple lights in your scenes relatively efficiently. There are many other lighting and shading techniques, and we'll look at many more of them in the rest of the book, starting with shadows and projection effects in the next chapter.

4
Projection and Shadowing Effects

Our `PrelightingRenderer` is a great way to render a large number of lights in a relatively efficient manner and it also makes a great framework for implementing some other fairly complicated effects. In this chapter, we will look at two related effects—*projective texturing* and *shadow mapping*. We saw some aspects of projective texturing in the last chapter, but in this chapter we will learn how to project an image across the scene as though it was projected by a real world projector.

Next, we will look at two implementations of shadow mapping. Shadow mapping is similar to projective texturing—in that we use the same process to project a depth texture across the scene, which we then use to generate shadows. However, the process is limited to hard-edged shadows, so we will look at a second way to perform shadow mapping that allows us to blur the depth texture and achieve soft shadows.

Projective texturing

Projective texturing is a technique that "projects" a texture across the scene, as though it were an image being projected onto the objects in a room by a real-world projector. This is useful for simulating effects such as video projectors or non-circular spot lights, and the process (as we shall see later in the chapter) can be extended to support what is called **shadow mapping**—a way to add shadows to the objects in our scenes.

In this example, our projector will be placed at one position and will point towards a target position. A texture will be projected toward the target position and appear on any objects that lie in its path:

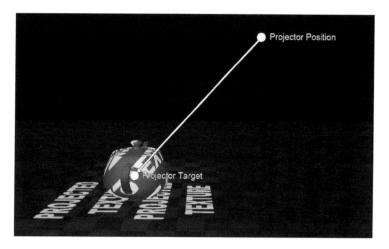

The projective texturing process is fairly simple and, in fact, we have been doing it since the last chapter. In the last chapter, we looked up the normal, depth, and lighting values for various pixels in our pixel shaders by finding the screen space positions of the geometry being shaded at those pixels, and then sampling our various texture maps at those pixel coordinates. The only difference with projective texturing is that we use different view and projection matrices when calculating that screen space position—in this case, we calculate the view and projection matrices for a virtual "camera" at the projector's position pointing towards its target. We then take the screen space position of our vertices and look up the corresponding pixel colors in the texture we are projecting. Finally, we add those colors to the pixel shader's output.

The first thing we will need is a new `Material` class to store the projector settings:

```
public class ProjectedTextureMaterial : Material
{
  public Vector3 ProjectorPosition { get; set; }
  public Vector3 ProjectorTarget { get; set; }
  public Texture2D ProjectedTexture { get; set; }
  public bool ProjectorEnabled { get; set; }
  public float Scale { get; set; }

  float halfWidth, halfHeight;

  public ProjectedTextureMaterial(Texture2D Texture,
```

```
      GraphicsDevice graphicsDevice)
{

    ProjectorPosition = new Vector3(1500, 1500, 1500);
    ProjectorTarget = new Vector3(0, 150, 0);
    ProjectorEnabled = true;
    ProjectedTexture = Texture;

    // We determine how large the texture will be based on the
    // texture dimensions and a scaling value
    halfWidth = Texture.Width / 2.0f;
    halfHeight = Texture.Height / 2.0f;
    Scale = 1;
}

public override void SetEffectParameters(Effect effect)
{
    if (effect.Parameters["ProjectorEnabled"] != null)
      effect.Parameters["ProjectorEnabled"].SetValue(
        ProjectorEnabled);

    if (!ProjectorEnabled)
      return;

    // Calculate an orthographic projection matrix for the
     // projector "camera"
      Matrix projection = Matrix.CreateOrthographicOffCenter(
        -halfWidth * Scale, halfWidth * Scale,
        -halfHeight * Scale, halfHeight * Scale,
        -100000, 100000);

    // Calculate view matrix as usual
    Matrix view = Matrix.CreateLookAt(ProjectorPosition,
     ProjectorTarget, Vector3.Up);

    if (effect.Parameters["ProjectorViewProjection"] != null)
      effect.Parameters["ProjectorViewProjection"].SetValue(
        view * projection);

    if (effect.Parameters["ProjectedTexture"] != null)
      effect.Parameters["ProjectedTexture"].SetValue(
        ProjectedTexture);
  }
}
```

Note that the projection matrix that this material generates is different from those that our cameras have been using—in that this matrix is **orthographic**. When a scene is viewed with an orthographic camera, objects do not appear to get smaller as their distance from the camera decreases. This is perfect for projective texturing, as the *rays* our projector casts will all be parallel:

Keep in mind that while we are using an orthographic projection matrix for this example; we could easily use a perspective projection matrix to achieve an effect more like a real-world projector (where moving the projector away from the screen would make the image larger because the rays it casts diverge from the center rather than remaining parallel).

The next step is to create an effect for projective texturing. To allow us to use the lighting system that we are used to, we will build a new effect based on the PPModel.fx effect. Start by copying that effect, and then add the following effect parameters. The parameters represent the view and projection matrices that our virtual "projector" is using, and which texture we would like to project:

```
float4x4 ProjectorViewProjection;

texture2D ProjectedTexture;
sampler2D projectorSampler = sampler_state
{
    texture = <ProjectedTexture>;
};

bool ProjectorEnabled = false;
```

Our vertex shader output `struct` will need one more field to store the screen space position of our vertices according to the `ProjectorViewProjection` matrix:

```
struct VertexShaderOutput
{
  float4 Position : POSITION0;
  float2 UV : TEXCOORD0;
  float4 PositionCopy : TEXCOORD1;
  float4 ProjectorScreenPosition : TEXCOORD2;
};
```

Then, our vertex shader will need to calculate this value:

```
output.ProjectorScreenPosition = mul(mul(input.Position, World),
    ProjectorViewProjection);
```

The last step is to sample from the texture that we would like to project. However, we cannot simply use the UV coordinates calculated from the screen space position, as we may be shading vertices outside of the range of our projected texture (that is, the vertices the projected image is not meant to fall on to.) To solve this problem, we need to return only a texture sample if the point being sampled is visible to the projector, by limiting UV coordinates to [0, 1] and [0, 1]. Outside of that range we will simply use black, so that nothing is added to the output color:

```
float3 sampleProjector(float2 UV)
{
  if (UV.x < 0 || UV.x > 1 || UV.y < 0 || UV.y > 1)
    return float3(0, 0, 0);

  return tex2D(projectorSampler, UV);
}
```

We can then use this new function to sample from the texture in the pixel shader:

```
light += AmbientColor;

float3 projection = float3(0, 0, 0);

if (ProjectorEnabled)
  projection = sampleProjector(postProjToScreen(
    input.ProjectorScreenPosition) + halfPixel());

return float4(basicTexture * DiffuseColor * light + projection, 1);
```

Finally, we can update our game to use the projective texturing effect and material:

```
Effect effect = Content.Load<Effect>("ProjectedTexture");

models[0].SetModelEffect(effect, true);
models[1].SetModelEffect(effect, true);

ProjectedTextureMaterial mat = new ProjectedTextureMaterial(
    Content.Load<Texture2D>("projected texture"), GraphicsDevice);
mat.ProjectorPosition = new Vector3(0, 4500, 4500);
mat.ProjectorTarget = new Vector3(0, 0, 0);
mat.Scale = 2;

models[0].Material = mat;
models[1].Material = mat;
```

Shadow mapping—drawing the depth map

Now that we've seen how to perform projective texturing, we are ready to learn how to add shadows to our scene with **shadow mapping**. Shadow mapping is a process where we:

1. Render the scene to a **depth texture**. This is similar to the depth texture we rendered to perform prelighting, but this time we render the scene from the light's point of view, pretending that the light we are generating shadows for is a point-target type of camera. The depth texture will store the distance from the light of the closest vertices that are in view of the light's virtual camera.

2. Render the scene using the normal effects, but project the depth texture onto the scene from the light's point of view. This will allow us to extract the depth value in the depth texture for each vertex that we shade.

3. Calculate the actual distance between each vertex and the light. We can then compare the value stored in the depth texture and the actual distance. If the actual distance between a vertex and the light is greater than the distance stored in the depth texture, then there must have been another vertex between it and the light that overwrote the original vertex's depth value. Therefore, the vertex we are currently shading must be obscured from the light's point of view and therefore, is in shadow.

4. If a vertex is in shadow, we multiply its final color value by some amount to darken the areas that are in shadow.

The first step is to render the scene as a depth texture from the light's point of view. We did something similar in the previous chapter with our depth/normal buffer; however, that was rendered from the camera's point of view. The depth buffer we will render uses only the red component of the color output, in order to store depth with the full 32-bit accuracy afforded by disregarding the green, blue, and alpha channels. The distance from the camera is divided by a certain far-plane distance to get a number between 0 and 1, which can then be returned as the color value:

Let's start by writing a shader that will do this for us. The shader simply calculates the screen space position of each vertex as usual, and calculates the depth (distance from the camera) of each vertex in the pixel shader. It then returns that value divided by the far plane and clamped to return a value between 0 and 1, where 0 would represent a vertex on the camera's near plane, and 1 would represent a vertex on the camera's far plane.

```
float4x4 World;
float4x4 View;
float4x4 Projection;

float FarPlane = 10000;

struct VertexShaderInput
{
    float4 Position : POSITION0;
};

struct VertexShaderOutput
{
    float4 Position : POSITION0;
    float4 ScreenPosition : TEXCOORD0;
};

VertexShaderOutput VertexShaderFunction(VertexShaderInput input)
{
    VertexShaderOutput output;

    // Calculate the screen space position
    float4x4 wvp = mul(World, mul(View, Projection));
    float4 position = mul(input.Position, wvp);

    output.Position = position;
    output.ScreenPosition = position;

    return output;
}

float4 PixelShaderFunction(VertexShaderOutput input) : COLOR0
{
    // Determine the depth of this vertex / by the far plane distance,
    // limited to [0, 1]
    float depth = clamp(input.ScreenPosition.z / FarPlane, 0, 1);
```

```
    // Return only the depth value
    return float4(depth, 0, 0, 1);
}


technique Technique1
{
  pass Pass1
  {
    VertexShader = compile vs_1_1 VertexShaderFunction();
    PixelShader = compile ps_2_0 PixelShaderFunction();
  }
}
```

We now need to update our `PrelightingRenderer` class to draw this depth map during its draw cycle. First, we will need a number of new instance variables and properties:

```
// Position and target of the shadowing light
public Vector3 ShadowLightPosition { get; set; }
public Vector3 ShadowLightTarget { get; set; }

// Shadow depth target and depth-texture effect
RenderTarget2D shadowDepthTarg;
Effect shadowDepthEffect;

// Depth texture parameters
int shadowMapSize = 2048;
int shadowFarPlane = 10000;

// Shadow light view and projection
Matrix shadowView, shadowProjection;

// Shadow properties
public bool DoShadowMapping { get; set; }
public float ShadowMult { get; set; }
```

The depth texture target and the depth texture effect need to be initialized in the constructor:

```
shadowDepthTarg = new RenderTarget2D(GraphicsDevice, shadowMapSize,
    shadowMapSize, false, SurfaceFormat.Single, DepthFormat.Depth24);

shadowDepthEffect = Content.Load<Effect>("ShadowDepthEffect");
shadowDepthEffect.Parameters["FarPlane"].SetValue(shadowFarPlane);
```

Next, we'll need a function to render the depth map:

```
void drawShadowDepthMap()
{
  // Calculate view and projection matrices for the "light"
  // shadows are being calculated for
  shadowView = Matrix.CreateLookAt(ShadowLightPosition,
ShadowLightTarget,
      Vector3.Up);

  shadowProjection = Matrix.CreatePerspectiveFieldOfView(
      MathHelper.ToRadians(45), 1, 1, shadowFarPlane);

  // Set render target
  graphicsDevice.SetRenderTarget(shadowDepthTarg);

  // Clear the render target to 1 (infinite depth)
  graphicsDevice.Clear(Color.White);

  // Draw each model with the ShadowDepthEffect effect
  foreach (CModel model in Models)
  {
    model.CacheEffects();
    model.SetModelEffect(shadowDepthEffect, false);
    model.Draw(shadowView, shadowProjection, ShadowLightPosition);
    model.RestoreEffects();
  }

  // Un-set the render targets
  graphicsDevice.SetRenderTarget(null);
}
```

Finally, we must be sure to call this function from the Draw() function:

```
public void Draw()
{
  drawDepthNormalMap();
  drawLightMap();
  if (DoShadowMapping) drawShadowDepthMap();
  prepareMainPass();
}
```

Shadow mapping—projecting the depth texture onto the scene

The shadow mapping technique depends on the fact that the pixel shader shades only the vertices that are closest to the camera. Therefore, only the objects closest to the "light" will be drawn into the depth buffer when the scene is drawn from the light's point of view. When we are drawing our objects from the camera's point of view, we can determine each vertex's actual distance from the light source, which we can then compare to the value stored in the depth buffer. If the value stored in the depth buffer is lesser than the vertex's actual distance from the light source, it must have an object between it and the camera and must therefore, be in shadow:

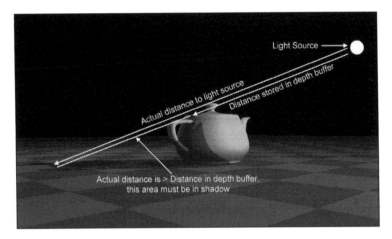

In order to get the value stored in the depth map for a given pixel, we will project the depth map onto the scene exactly the same way we did in the previous example. We will be adding the shadowing code to another extension of the PPModel.fx effect, so begin by copying that effect and adding the parameters we will need to project the texture onto the scene:

```
bool DoShadowMapping = true;
float4x4 ShadowView;
float4x4 ShadowProjection;

texture2D ShadowMap;
sampler2D shadowSampler = sampler_state {
    texture = <ShadowMap>;
    minfilter = point;
    magfilter = point;
    mipfilter = point;
};
```

Our `VertexShaderOutput` struct will need new values as well—the screen space position of the vertex as seen by the light:

```
float4 ShadowScreenPosition : TEXCOORD2;
```

The vertex shader will then need to calculate this value:

```
output.ShadowScreenPosition = mul(mul(input.Position, World),
    mul(ShadowView, ShadowProjection));
```

Now, we will need to sample from the depth texture. Once again, we must be careful to sample from the texture only when the UV coordinates are in the [0, 1] range, otherwise there will not be a smooth transition between those areas that the virtual light camera can see.

```
float sampleShadowMap(float2 UV)
{
   if (UV.x < 0 || UV.x > 1 || UV.y < 0 || UV.y > 1)
     return 1;

   return tex2D(shadowSampler, UV).r;
}
```

Finally, we can use this function to sample from the depth texture in the pixel shader:

```
float2 shadowTexCoord = postProjToScreen(input.ShadowScreenPosition)
    + halfPixel();

float mapDepth = sampleShadowMap(shadowTexCoord);
```

If we were to return this value alone, we would be projecting the depth texture onto the scene:

```
return float4(mapDepth, mapDepth, mapDepth, 1);
```

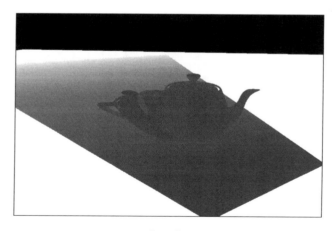

Before we actually use this depth value to generate shadows, we need to be sure that we are setting all of the effect parameters that we just added in the `prepareMainPass()` function of `PrelightingRenderer`:

```
if (part.Effect.Parameters["DoShadowMapping"] != null)
  part.Effect.Parameters["DoShadowMapping"].SetValue(DoShadowMapping);

if (!DoShadowMapping) continue;

if (part.Effect.Parameters["ShadowMap"] != null)
  part.Effect.Parameters["ShadowMap"].SetValue(shadowDepthTarg);

if (part.Effect.Parameters["ShadowView"] != null)
  part.Effect.Parameters["ShadowView"].SetValue(shadowView);

if (part.Effect.Parameters["ShadowProjection"] != null)
  part.Effect.Parameters["ShadowProjection"].
    SetValue(shadowProjection);
```

Shadow mapping—performing the depth comparison

The final step in shadow mapping is to compare the depth value stored in the depth texture to the actual distance between each vertex and the camera. We will need three more effect parameters to calculate and compare depth values and to perform the final shading in the pixel shader:

```
float3 ShadowLightPosition;
float ShadowFarPlane;
float ShadowMult = 0.3f;
float ShadowBias = 1.0f / 50.0f;
```

The last parameter is what is called the **depth bias**. Remember that we are comparing a relatively precise actual distance between each vertex and the light to a distance that has been stored in a texture. Because that texture is limited in size and precision, the depth value that we will get when sampling from it will be somewhat inaccurate. If we tried to compare that value to the actual distance we calculated directly, we would end up with very messy shadows on some surfaces, instead of a smoothly transitioning shadow:

In the case of the previous screenshot, the surface of the teapot is curved, which leads to banding where the depth texture had stored somewhat inaccurate depth values. Notice also that the floor is entirely in shadow in this image—another flaw caused by the depth texture's lack of precision.

We solve this problem with the depth bias, by subtracting a small amount from the actual depth before comparing it to the value stored in the depth texture. A large enough bias will reduce these flaws, but may also cause a lack of shadows on steep enough surfaces. Finding the right depth bias is more of an art than a science, and there are other techniques available (using a *slope-scaled depth bias* for example), but for simplicity's sake, we will use a constant bias. Increasing the size of the depth texture will also help to reduce these errors.

We perform the depth comparison as follows—multiplying the output color by the shadow darkness, if we determine the area to be in shadow:

```
float2 shadowTexCoord = postProjToScreen(input.ShadowScreenPosition)
    + halfPixel();

float mapDepth = sampleShadowMap(shadowTexCoord);
```

```
float realDepth = input.ShadowScreenPosition.z / ShadowFarPlane;
float shadow = 1;

if (realDepth < 1 && realDepth - ShadowBias > mapDepth)
  shadow = ShadowMult;

return float4(basicTexture * DiffuseColor * light * shadow, 1);
```

We will also need to be sure to set our new `Effect` parameters in the `PrelightingRenderer` class:

```
if (part.Effect.Parameters["ShadowLightPosition"] != null)
  part.Effect.Parameters["ShadowLightPosition"].
    SetValue(ShadowLightPosition);

if (part.Effect.Parameters["ShadowFarPlane"] != null)
  part.Effect.Parameters["ShadowFarPlane"].SetValue(shadowFarPlane);

if (part.Effect.Parameters["ShadowMult"] != null)
  part.Effect.Parameters["ShadowMult"].SetValue(ShadowMult);
```

Finally, we set up the renderer to generate shadows in the `Game1` class:

```
renderer.ShadowLightPosition = new Vector3(1500, 1500, 2000);
renderer.ShadowLightTarget = new Vector3(0, 150, 0);
renderer.DoShadowMapping = true;
renderer.ShadowMult = 0.3f;
```

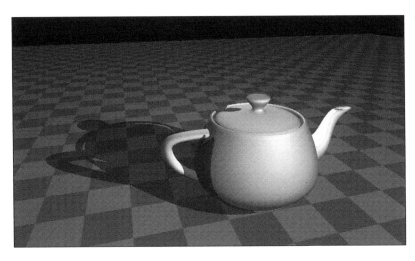

Variance shadow mapping—soft shadows

Our current shadows look nice, but they do not behave like those found in the real world. While shadows often do have sharp edges, most of the time they do not. On overcast days, or when objects are hit with an indirect light source, shadows will often appear fuzzy and blurry. In the following sections, we will implement **soft shadows** with a technique called **Variance Shadow Maps** (**VSM**). The major benefit of variance shadow mapping is that we can filter the depth texture like a regular texture—in this case, blurring it—without ruining the shadows that result.

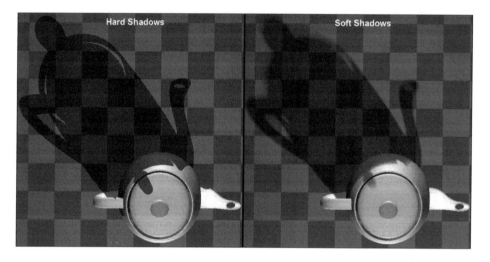

This section will focus more on the implementation of VSM, but the original paper and presentation for the technique as well as another example implementation are available at `http://www.punkuser.net/vsm`.

The first difference between "regular" shadow mapping and VSM is that we store both the depth and the square of the depth in the depth texture. We later use these values to approximate shadows. First, we will need to update the depth texture rendering effect to return both of these values:

```
return float4(depth, depth * depth, 0, 1);
```

Now that our depth texture effect is returning two values, we need to change the surface format that we are using. In the past, we've used `SurfaceFormat.Single`, which is a 32-bit format with all 32 bits allocated to the red channel. This allows us to store relatively precise depth values in the red channel of a render target—much more precise than `SurfaceFormat.Color` for example, which allocates only 8 bits to the red channel.

Because we are now storing two values, we will use `SurfaceFormat.HalfVector2`. This is also a 32-bit format, allocating 16 bits to the red channel and 16 bits to the green channel. This is less precise than what we have been using, but because we are blurring the shadow map the difference is not very noticeable. This will allow us to keep memory requirements down, especially given the number of render targets we have accumulated.

```
shadowDepthTarg = new RenderTarget2D(GraphicsDevice, shadowMapSize,
    shadowMapSize, false, SurfaceFormat.HalfVector2,
    DepthFormat.Depth24);
```

Variance shadow mapping—blurring the depth texture

The next step in the VSM process is to blur the depth texture that we just rendered, using what is called a **Gaussian blur**. *Chapter 8* covers Gaussian blurs in much more detail, but for simplicity's sake, we will use pre-calculated settings for the blur. Blurring the depth texture will give us soft shadows. If we did not blur the depth texture at all, we would get shadows nearly identical to those we created earlier.

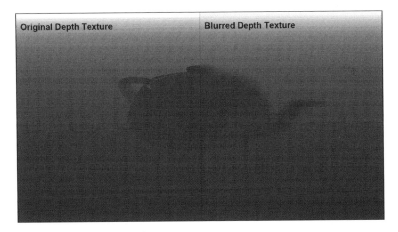

Blurring is simply the process of averaging a pixel and its neighbors for every pixel in the image—"smoothing" out the image as a whole. The Gaussian blur improves this somewhat by using specific pixel offsets and weights but the process is the same. The Gaussian blur effect is as follows:

```
// The texture to blur
texture ScreenTexture;

sampler2D tex = sampler_state {
```

```
    texture = <ScreenTexture>;
    minfilter = point;
    magfilter = point;
    mipfilter = point;
};

// Precalculated weights and offsets
float weights[15] = { 0.1061154, 0.1028506, 0.1028506, 0.09364651,
    0.09364651, 0.0801001, 0.0801001, 0.06436224, 0.06436224,
    0.04858317, 0.04858317, 0.03445063, 0.03445063, 0.02294906,
    0.02294906 };

float offsets[15] = { 0, 0.00125, -0.00125, 0.002916667,
    -0.002916667, 0.004583334, -0.004583334, 0.00625, -0.00625,
    0.007916667, -0.007916667, 0.009583334, -0.009583334, 0.01125,
    -0.01125 };

// Blurs the input image horizontally
float4 BlurHorizontal(float4 Position : POSITION0,
    float2 UV : TEXCOORD0) : COLOR0
{
  float4 output = float4(0, 0, 0, 1);

  // Sample from the surrounding pixels using the precalculated
  // pixel offsets and color weights
  for (int i = 0; i < 15; i++)
    output += tex2D(tex, UV + float2(offsets[i], 0)) * weights[i];

  return output;
}

// Blurs the input image vertically
float4 BlurVertical(float4 Position : POSITION0,
    float2 UV : TEXCOORD0) : COLOR0
{
  float4 output = float4(0, 0, 0, 1);

  for (int i = 0; i < 15; i++)
    output += tex2D(tex, UV + float2(0, offsets[i])) * weights[i];

  return output;
}

technique Technique1
{
```

```
pass Horizontal
{
    PixelShader = compile ps_2_0 BlurHorizontal();
}

pass Vertical
{
    PixelShader = compile ps_2_0 BlurVertical();
}
}
```

Notice that this effect contains two techniques—one for blurring the image horizontally and one for blurring vertically. We blur each direction independently to create a smoother blur. Notice also that each pixel shader simply adds the contributions of 15 neighboring pixels and averages the result as discussed earlier.

For the `PrelightingRenderer` class to perform the blur, we will need a few more instance variables—a `SpriteBatch` to draw the depth map into render targets, the Gaussian blur effect, and a render target where we will store the result of the horizontal blur. We blur vertically using the original depth buffer as the target, sampling the horizontally blurred scene from this secondary render target.

```
SpriteBatch spriteBatch;
RenderTarget2D shadowBlurTarg;
Effect shadowBlurEffect;
```

These values need to be initialized in the constructor:

```
spriteBatch = new SpriteBatch(GraphicsDevice);
shadowBlurEffect = Content.Load<Effect>("GaussianBlur");

shadowBlurTarg = new RenderTarget2D(GraphicsDevice, shadowMapSize,
    shadowMapSize, false, SurfaceFormat.Color, DepthFormat.Depth24);
```

Next, we'll create the function that performs the blur. Notice that we specify which render target to sample from and which render target to draw into. We also specify which technique we'd like to use with the `dir` parameter—0 for the horizontal blur technique and 1 for the vertical blur technique.

```
void blurShadow(RenderTarget2D to, RenderTarget2D from, int dir)
{
    // Set the target render target
    graphicsDevice.SetRenderTarget(to);

    graphicsDevice.Clear(Color.Black);
```

```
        spriteBatch.Begin(SpriteSortMode.Immediate, BlendState.Opaque);

        // Start the Gaussian blur effect
        shadowBlurEffect.CurrentTechnique.Passes[dir].Apply();

        // Draw the contents of the source render target so they can
        // be blurred by the gaussian blur pixel shader
        spriteBatch.Draw(from, Vector2.Zero, Color.White);

        spriteBatch.End();

        // Clean up after the sprite batch
        graphicsDevice.BlendState = BlendState.Opaque;
        graphicsDevice.DepthStencilState = DepthStencilState.Default;

        // Remove the render target
        graphicsDevice.SetRenderTarget(null);
    }
```

In the last change to the `PrelightingRenderer` class, we need to be sure to blur the shadow in the `Draw()` function. Notice that we first copy from the depth target to the blur target, blurring horizontally along the way, then copy from the blur target back to the depth target, blurring vertically along the way.

```
    public void Draw()
    {
      drawDepthNormalMap();
      drawLightMap();

      if (DoShadowMapping)
      {
        drawShadowDepthMap();
        blurShadow(shadowBlurTarg, shadowDepthTarg, 0);
        blurShadow(shadowDepthTarg, shadowBlurTarg, 1);
      }

      prepareMainPass();
    }
```

Variance shadow mapping—generating shadows

The last step in variance shadow mapping is to generate the shadows themselves. We will do this in the same place where we calculated the shadows in the previous example. As we are now storing two values in the depth texture, we first need to update our sampling function to return the red and green values:

```
float2 sampleShadowMap(float2 UV)
{
  if (UV.x < 0 || UV.x > 1 || UV.y < 0 || UV.y > 1)
    return float2(1, 1);

  return tex2D(shadowSampler, UV).rg;
}
```

Finally, we can update the pixel shader to do the variance shadow mapping calculations. We sample from the depth texture as usual to get the depth it contains, and calculate the light distance as usual, offsetting it with a small bias. From there, we perform the shadow calculations as demonstrated in the VSM example code:

```
float shadow = 1;

if (DoShadowMapping)
{
  float2 shadowTexCoord = postProjToScreen(input.ShadowScreenPosition)
    + halfPixel();

  float realDepth = input.ShadowScreenPosition.z / ShadowFarPlane
    - ShadowBias;

  if (realDepth < 1)
  {
    // Variance shadow mapping code below from the variance shadow
    // mapping demo code @ http://www.punkuser.net/vsm/

    // Sample from depth texture
    float2 moments = sampleShadowMap(shadowTexCoord);

    // Check if we're in shadow
    float lit_factor = (realDepth <= moments.x);

    // Variance shadow mapping
    float E_x2 = moments.y;
```

```
        float Ex_2 = moments.x * moments.x;
        float variance = min(max(E_x2 - Ex_2, 0.0) +
                1.0f / 10000.0f, 1.0);
        float m_d = (moments.x - realDepth);
        float p = variance / (variance + m_d * m_d);

        shadow = clamp(max(lit_factor, p), ShadowMult, 1.0f);
    }
}

    return float4(basicTexture * DiffuseColor * light * shadow, 1);
```

Summary

Now that you've finished this chapter, you've learned how to use projective texturing to project 2D images onto your 3D scenes. You've also learned how to extend the projective texturing effect to project depth textures onto the scene. You then learned how to use that depth texture to calculate both hard- and soft- edged shadows. In the next chapter, we will look at a number of "shader effects". These are effects that involve shaders but are not strictly lighting effects—reflections, fog, and so on.

5
Shader Effects

HLSL provides us with an incredible amount of power when it comes to what I call **shader effects**. These special effects are carried out by the vertex and pixel shaders on the graphics card rather than through some other method on the CPU. Because the GPU works directly with vertices and pixels, it can perform certain tasks such as per pixel lighting, shadow mapping, and so on—as we've already seen—easily and extremely efficiently. In this chapter, we will implement a number of these "3D effects" in our own game, and gain an understanding of how powerful these effects can be.

We will look at four effects: fog, normal mapping, cube mapping, and a water effect. **Fog** is used to hide the scene after a given distance. This can have both dramatic and practical effects: we don't need to draw objects after a certain distance, if we have faded to the fog color before seeing them, for example. **Normal mapping** is used to provide extra detail to a surface without adding more polygons and vertices. **Cube mapping** is an effect that is used to add reflections to objects. Although these reflections can be generated in real time, this is very inefficient using the cube mapping technique, so we will look at cube mapping with existing 3D textures. Finally, we will create a **water effect** that will actually generate reflections in real time, reflecting the environment around the water as it changes.

Fog

Fog can be entirely implemented in an effect—all we need to do is determine the distance from the camera of each vertex that we are shading and fade the final color to a given fog color based on that distance. We will base this effect on the `LightingEffect` effect by making a copy of that effect. We will then add the following `effect` parameters:

```
float FogStart = 2000;
float FogEnd = 10000;
float3 FogColor = float3(1, 1, 1);
```

Finally, we can just do some very simple blending in the pixel shader based on how far away the point we are shading is:

```
// Calculate fog amount
float dist = length(input.ViewDirection);
float fog = clamp((dist - FogStart) / (FogEnd - FogStart), 0, 1);

return float4(lerp(output, FogColor, fog), 1);
```

Applying the fog effect to our models will yield the following result:

Normal mapping

The first effect that we are going to cover is called **normal mapping**. You may recall from earlier chapters that a polygon's "normal" is the vector pointing directly away from (perpendicular to) the polygon's surface.

We use this normal when calculating lighting, where the amount of diffuse lighting for a given polygon is the dot product of the polygon's normal and the light direction. Until now, we have relied on the model file itself to give us each vertex's normal vector, but there are other more creative ways to obtain a normal.

The following screenshot depicts a flat rectangle with a brick texture applied to it. Because the wall is flat, there is only one normal vector and it points directly away from the wall. We can imagine that this will produce flat lighting across the entire wall, despite the fact that a real brick wall varies across its surface due to the bumps and valleys its bricks create on its surface:

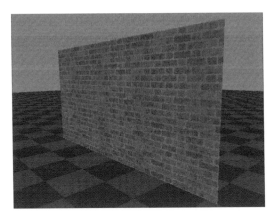

What if, instead of using the model's built-in normal vector, we sampled normal values as the RGB values of a second texture mapped to its surface?

If we were to take the (R, G, B) values and map them to a [-1, 1] range, we could effectively extract the normal for each pixel the wall covers. The texture we are sampling from is called a **normal map**, and this process is called normal mapping. Notice in the previous screenshot that the normal map appears to line up with the texture shown in the next screenshot, although the normal map looks a little odd as it is really storing three pieces of information (the X, Y, and Z components of the normal) in every pixel.

If we sample the normal map to construct normals instead of using the normals built into the model, the wall can appear to have much more detail without the need for a ton of extra vertices:

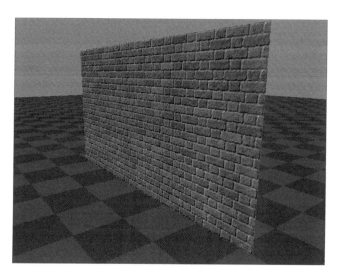

This is the same model and the same texture. The only difference is that the normals have been extracted from the normal map rather than from the model. This is an extremely fast way of vastly improving the apparent quality of a model. This is one of the most common 3D effects used in modern videogames, so it's well worth learning. That said, let's get to it!

The normal mapping effect will be based on the `LightEffect.fx` effect, so begin by copying that effect. We will simply be substituting the use of the model's normal with the use of the normal extracted from a normal map. First, we need to add a parameter for the normal map and its sampler:

```
texture NormalMap;

sampler NormalMapSampler = sampler_state {
    texture = <NormalMap>;
    MinFilter = Anisotropic;
    MagFilter = Anisotropic;
    MipFilter = Linear;
    AddressU = Wrap;
    AddressV = Wrap;
};
```

Next, we will go ahead and remove the original normal calculations from the vertex shader and its input/output structs:

```
struct VertexShaderInput
{
  float4 Position : POSITION0;
  float2 UV : TEXCOORD0;
};

struct VertexShaderOutput
{
  float4 Position : POSITION0;
  float2 UV : TEXCOORD0;
  float3 ViewDirection : TEXCOORD2;
};

VertexShaderOutput VertexShaderFunction(VertexShaderInput input)
{
  VertexShaderOutput output;

  float4 worldPosition = mul(input.Position, World);
  float4x4 viewProjection = mul(View, Projection);
  output.Position = mul(worldPosition, viewProjection);
```

```
output.UV = input.UV;

output.ViewDirection = worldPosition - CameraPosition;

return output;
}
```

Finally, we can update the lighting section of the pixel shader to extract the normals from our normal map and use them for the lighting calculations:

```
// Start with ambient lighting
float3 lighting = AmbientColor;

float3 lightDir = normalize(LightDirection);

// Extract the normals from the normal map
float3 normal = tex2D(NormalMapSampler, input.UV).rgb;
normal = normal * 2 - 1; // Move from [0, 1] to [-1, 1] range

// Add lambertian lighting
lighting += saturate(dot(lightDir, normal)) * LightColor;
```

Next, we'll create a new material based on the `LightMaterial` class that will keep track of the normal map for us:

```
public class NormalMapMaterial : LightingMaterial
{
    public Texture2D NormalMap { get; set; }

    public NormalMapMaterial(Texture2D NormalMap)
    {
        this.NormalMap = NormalMap;
    }

    public override void SetEffectParameters(Effect effect)
    {
        base.SetEffectParameters(effect);

        if (effect.Parameters["NormalMap"] != null)
            effect.Parameters["NormalMap"].SetValue(NormalMap);
    }
}
```

To demonstrate our new normal mapping effect, we'd set our scene up as follows:

```
models.Add(new CModel(Content.Load<Model>("ground"),
    Vector3.Zero, Vector3.Zero, Vector3.One, GraphicsDevice));

models.Add(new CModel(Content.Load<Model>("brick_wall"),
    Vector3.Zero, new Vector3(0,0, 0), Vector3.One, GraphicsDevice));

Effect lightingEffect = Content.Load<Effect>("LightingEffect");
LightingMaterial lightingMat = new LightingMaterial();
```

```
Effect normalMapEffect = Content.Load<Effect>("NormalMapEffect");
NormalMapMaterial normalMat = new NormalMapMaterial(
    Content.Load<Texture2D>("brick_normal_map"));

lightingMat.LightDirection = new Vector3(.5f, .5f, 1);
lightingMat.LightColor = Vector3.One;

normalMat.LightDirection = new Vector3(.5f, .5f, 1);
normalMat.LightColor = Vector3.One;

models[0].SetModelEffect(lightingEffect, true);
models[1].SetModelEffect(normalMapEffect, true);

models[0].Material = lightingMat;
models[1].Material = normalMat;
```

Generating normal maps with Photoshop

The "correct" way to generate normal maps for a model is to build two versions of the model—a high resolution version and another version that is of a lower resolution (fewer vertices). From there, the modeling tool will generate normal maps that, when applied to the lower resolution model, will approximate the appearance of the higher resolution model. In this way, a similar level of detail can be achieved while the total number of polygons drawn is reduced. This process is different for every modeling tool, however, and is beyond the scope of this book, so it will not be covered here. However, there is another way to generate normal maps using Adobe Photoshop that can still improve the appearance of your models.

We are going to generate a normal map for the brick wall that we have been using thus far. The final result will not be as good as the "real" normal map we have been using, but it will still make the wall look more detailed and won't require us to build our own models for the wall. To start with, you will need Adobe Photoshop—it is an expensive software but you may be able to get it for a lower price if you are a student, or if you work for a graphics company, and so on. There are other tools available that can also create normal maps from textures, but we will focus on Photoshop in this book as the general process remains the same. Once you have Photoshop, you will need to download and install the "NVIDIA Plug-ins for Adobe Photoshop" from `http://developer.nvidia.com/object/photoshop_dds_plugins.html`. This package contains the tools needed to create normal maps from images and to create DirectX's `.dds` image files.

To start, open the texture file in Photoshop. Then, choose **Image | Adjustments | Desaturate** to remove the color from the image.

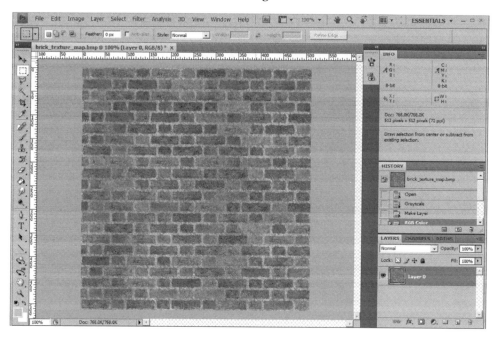

Next, invert the image (*Ctrl + I*) to swap white and black colors in the image. This will turn the image into a height map, where pixels with a color value of zero indicate the lowest height, and pixels with the color value of one indicate the highest area of the image. You can imagine our bricks as "bumps" on the height map, where the valleys between them are darker and the bricks themselves are lighter. Next, use the **Image | Adjustments | Brightness** and **Contrast** menu to make the difference between lighter and darker areas more dramatic. You will probably need to do this multiple times to achieve the desired effect.

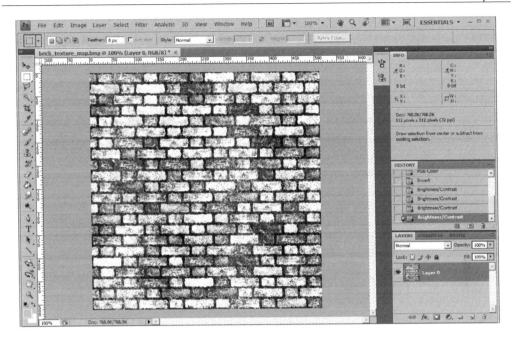

Finally, we can use the normal map filter under **Filter | NVIDIA Tools | NormalMapFilter** to convert our height map into a normal map. Ensure that under **Height Generation**, **Filter Type** is set to **3x3**, **Invert Y** is checked, **Scale** is set to **10**, and **Height Source** is set to **Average RGB**. Choosing these settings is more of a guess and check process than a science—the goal is to make something that looks good in the end. In this case, **Average RGB** will cause the plugin to use the color value as the height.

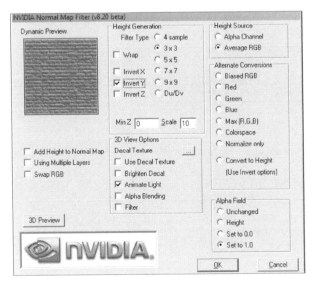

NVIDIA's tool will then convert your image into a normal map.

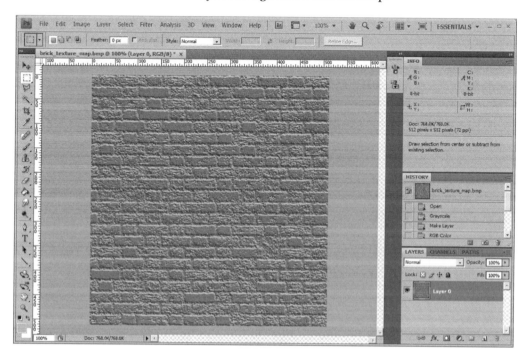

If you were to save this normal map and load it instead onto your brick wall texture, you would see that while this normal map is not as "correct" as the other, it still does a good job of approximating the brick pattern:

Cube mapping: Making a sky sphere

The second effect we will discuss is called **cube mapping**. A **cube map** is like a texture, but it actually contains six textures—one for each side of a cube:

Cube mapping is any process that involves sampling pixels from this texture. In the following sections, we will use the preceding cube map to simulate reflections off of an object, and to simulate a sky wrapped around the scene. Let's start with the sky.

We start by creating a new class `SkySphere` that keeps track of a model and an effect. The model is simply a sphere that our cube map will be drawn onto, and the effect (which we will create next) does that drawing. We draw the sphere around the camera with the depth buffer disabled, so that the texture drawn on the inside of the sphere will "fake" an infinitely far away background:

```
public class SkySphere : IRenderable
{
  CModel model;
  Effect effect;
  GraphicsDevice graphics;

  public SkySphere(ContentManager Content,
      GraphicsDevice GraphicsDevice, TextureCube Texture)
  {
    model = new CModel(Content.Load<Model>("skysphere_mesh"),
        Vector3.Zero,Vector3.Zero, new Vector3(100000),
        GraphicsDevice);

    effect = Content.Load<Effect>("skysphere_effect");
    effect.Parameters["CubeMap"].SetValue(Texture);
```

```
        model.SetModelEffect(effect, false);

        this.graphics = GraphicsDevice;
    }
    public void Draw(Matrix View, Matrix Projection,
     Vector3 CameraPosition)
    {
        // Disable the depth buffer
        graphics.DepthStencilState = DepthStencilState.None;

        // Move the model with the sphere
        model.Position = CameraPosition;

        model.Draw(View, Projection, CameraPosition);

        graphics.DepthStencilState = DepthStencilState.Default;
    }
    public void SetClipPlane(Vector4? Plane)
    {
      effect.Parameters["ClipPlaneEnabled"].SetValue(Plane.HasValue);

      if (Plane.HasValue)
        effect.Parameters["ClipPlane"].SetValue(Plane.Value);
    }
}
```

Now we can create the effect. The effect parameters are fairly standard, except that we use a `samplerCUBE` parameter instead of a `sampler2D`:

```
float4x4 World;
float4x4 View;
float4x4 Projection;
float3 CameraPosition;

texture CubeMap;

samplerCUBE CubeMapSampler = sampler_state {
    texture = <CubeMap>;
    minfilter = anisotropic;
    magfilter = anisotropic;
};
```

The vertex shader simply outputs the regular position value and a copy of the world position:

```
struct VertexShaderInput
{
  float4 Position : POSITION0;
};
```

```
struct VertexShaderOutput
{
  float4 Position : POSITION0;
  float3 WorldPosition : TEXCOORD0;
};
VertexShaderOutput VertexShaderFunction(VertexShaderInput input)
{
  VertexShaderOutput output;
  float4 worldPosition = mul(input.Position, World);
  output.WorldPosition = worldPosition;
   output.Position = mul(worldPosition, mul(View, Projection));
  return output;
}
```

Finally, the pixel shader samples from the cube map. When sampling from a cube map, we use a vector as the texture coordinates—in this case, the vector from the camera to the surface of the sphere:

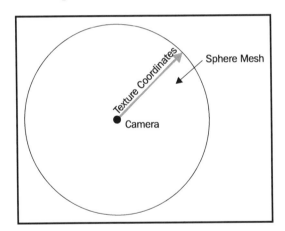

```
float4 PixelShaderFunction(VertexShaderOutput input) : COLOR0
{
  float3 viewDirection = normalize(input.WorldPosition -
    CameraPosition);
  return texCUBE(CubeMapSampler, viewDirection);
}
```

This effect has the standard technique definition:

```
technique Technique1
{
  pass Pass1
```

```
  {
    VertexShader = compile vs_2_0 VertexShaderFunction();
    PixelShader = compile ps_2_0 PixelShaderFunction();
  }
}
```

To implement the sky sphere into our game, we need an instance of the SkySphere class:

```
SkySphere sky;
```

This instance needs to be initialized in the LoadContent() function:

```
sky = new SkySphere(Content, GraphicsDevice,
    Content.Load<TextureCube>("clouds"));
```

Finally, we must be sure to call its Draw() function before anything else so it can be drawn as the infinitely far away background:

```
// Called when the game should draw itself
protected override void Draw(GameTime gameTime)
{
  GraphicsDevice.Clear(Color.CornflowerBlue);

  sky.Draw(camera.View, camera.Projection, (
    (FreeCamera)camera).Position);

  foreach (CModel model in models)
    if (camera.BoundingVolumeIsInView(model.BoundingSphere))
        model.Draw(camera.View, camera.Projection,
        ((FreeCamera)camera).Position);

  base.Draw(gameTime);
}
```

Cube mapping: Reflections

A second way to use cubemaps that we will now implement is to simulate reflections of the environment depicted in a cube map off of an object. To do this, we simply reflect the view direction off of the object's surface around its normal and use that vector as the texture coordinate. This simulates light bouncing off of the model's surface and entering the camera:

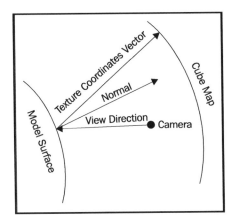

The HLSL shader is very simple — the only differences being that the vertex shader now outputs the normal and the view direction is reflected before being used to sample from the texture:

```
float4x4 World;
float4x4 View;
float4x4 Projection;
float3 CameraPosition;

texture CubeMap;

float4 ClipPlane;
bool ClipPlaneEnabled = false;

samplerCUBE CubeMapSampler = sampler_state {
   texture = <CubeMap>;
   minfilter = anisotropic;
   magfilter = anisotropic;
};

struct VertexShaderInput
{
   float4 Position : POSITION0;
   float3 Normal : NORMAL0;
};
```

```
struct VertexShaderOutput
{
  float4 Position : POSITION0;
  float3 WorldPosition : TEXCOORD0;
  float3 Normal : TEXCOORD1;
};

VertexShaderOutput VertexShaderFunction(VertexShaderInput input)
{
  VertexShaderOutput output;

  float4 worldPosition = mul(input.Position, World);
  output.WorldPosition = worldPosition;

  output.Position = mul(worldPosition, mul(View, Projection));

  output.Normal = mul(input.Normal, World);

  return output;
}

float4 PixelShaderFunction(VertexShaderOutput input) : COLOR0
{
  if (ClipPlaneEnabled)
    clip(dot(float4(input.WorldPosition, 1), ClipPlane));

  float3 viewDirection = normalize(
      input.WorldPosition - CameraPosition);
  float3 normal = normalize(input.Normal);

  // Reflect around normal
  float3 reflection = reflect(viewDirection, normal);

  return texCUBE(CubeMapSampler, reflection);
}

technique Technique1
{
  pass Pass1
  {
    VertexShader = compile vs_2_0 VertexShaderFunction();
    PixelShader = compile ps_2_0 PixelShaderFunction();
  }
}
```

The second and final step is to create a very simple material for this effect:

```
public class CubeMapReflectMaterial : Material
{
  public TextureCube CubeMap { get; set; }

  public CubeMapReflectMaterial(TextureCube CubeMap)
```

```
    {
        this.CubeMap = CubeMap;
    }
    public override void SetEffectParameters(Effect effect)
    {
        if (effect.Parameters["CubeMap"] != null)
            effect.Parameters["CubeMap"].SetValue(CubeMap);
    }
}
```

To use this new effect, we would add an object to our scene (in the LoadContent() method of the Game1 class) as follows:

```
models.Add(new CModel(Content.Load<Model>("teapot"),
    Vector3.Zero, Vector3.Zero, Vector3.One * 50, GraphicsDevice));

Effect cubeMapEffect = Content.Load<Effect>("CubeMapReflect");
CubeMapReflectMaterial cubeMat = new
    CubeMapReflectMaterial(Content.Load<TextureCube>("clouds"));

models[0].SetModelEffect(cubeMapEffect, false);
models[0].Material = cubeMat;
```

Rendering sky boxes with Terragen

There are many ways to create the cube map for a sky box. You can draw them by hand, render them from a 3D modeling program or the game itself, or, like we are going to do right now, render them with an environment modeling program such as Terragen. Terragen is a free program (unless you want to use it commercially, in which case you will need to pay $99) that renders terrain, water, and skies. We can specify the camera angles to render from in order to render the images for the six sides of our cube map.

The first step is to download and install Terragen. Download "Terragen Classic" from `http://planetside.co.uk`, install it, and launch the program. Before we render our environment, we need to set a few settings.

Let's begin with the general render settings.

1. Drag the slider under **Quality** all the way to 100%, and uncheck **Land**, as right now we only want to render the sky.

2. In the **Image Size** dialog, set the image size to the size you want. (512 pixels by 512 pixels is a good size, however the unregistered version of Terragen will allow you to export images up to 960 pixels wide and high for the highest quality sky.)

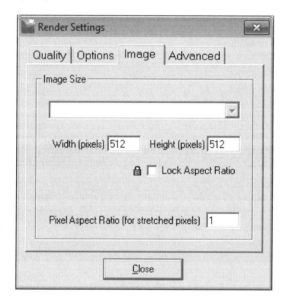

3. Next, set your camera settings. Under **Camera**, change the units to **Terrain Units**, and set the **Camera Position** to (**128, 128, 0**). Set the **Target Position** to (**128, 256, 0**) for now. Set both the **Fixed Height Above Surface** boxes to **0**.

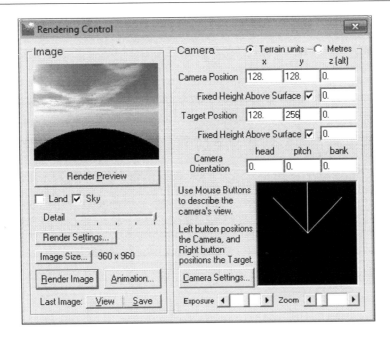

4. Finally, in the **Camera Settings** dialog, set the zoom level to 1.

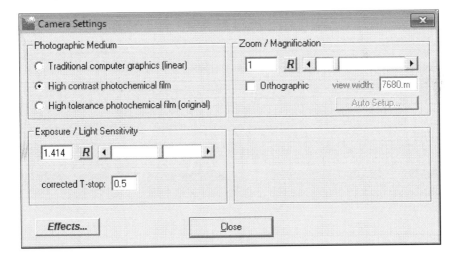

Now we can change the appearance of our sky. There are dozens of settings than can create all sorts of skies and landscapes, however for now I'm just going to focus on a standard cloudy blue sky. Click on the **Cloudscape** button on the toolbar on the left side of the screen.

We will first extend the height of our sky to cover more of the sky box, by setting the **Sky size** parameter. I set it to **8192** — twice its original height. Check **3D** to make Terragen render the clouds in 3D. Finally, adjust the contrast and density sliders as you see fit. In this case, I set them to 100 and 10 respectively.

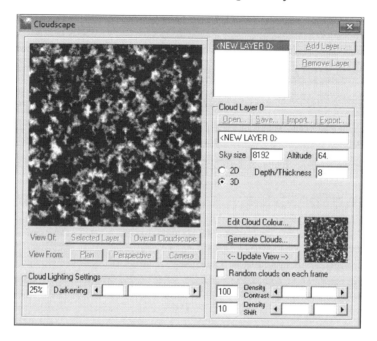

Finally, we can render our images by using the corresponding button on the **Rendering Control** pane. We need to render six times — one for each face of the cube map that will later be rendered around our scene. The **Save** button on the render window can be used to save each image when it finishes rendering. Render the following images with the respective camera target settings:

Image	Target X	Target Y	Target Z
Front.bmp	128	256	0
Right.bmp	256	128	0
Back.bmp	128	0	0
Left.bmp	0	128	0
Top.bmp	128	128	2
Bottom.bmp	128	128	-2

Now we need to combine these textures into a cube map. I've written a program to do just this. Download it from `http://www.innovativegames.net/blog/blog/2010/06/03/cubemapper` and run `CubeMapper.exe`. Specify the six input files and an output location for the cube map, then click on **Create Cube Map**. The program will generate your cube map for you, which you can then copy into your game's content directory and use as normal. Keep in mind that this program could also create cube maps from other textures—the source textures do not have to be from Terragen.

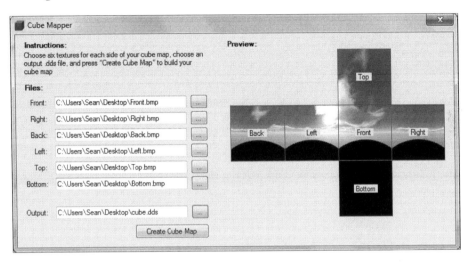

Creating a reflective water effect

The final example in this chapter will demonstrate how to create a water effect that reflects the environment above it. It will also make use of normal mapping to create a ripple effect, and we'll finish it off with some specular highlights.

Let's start with the basics. We'll need a class to represent our effect with a model and effect inside.

```
class Water
{
  CModel waterMesh;
  Effect waterEffect;

  ContentManager content;
  GraphicsDevice graphics;
  public WaterEffect(ContentManager content, GraphicsDevice graphics,
    Vector3 position, Vector2 size)
  {
    this.content = content;
    this.graphics = graphics;

    waterMesh = new CModel(content.Load<Model>("plane"), position,
        Vector3.Zero, new Vector3(size.X, 1, size.Y), graphics);

    waterEffect = content.Load<Effect>("WaterEffect");
    waterMesh.SetModelEffect(waterEffect, false);

    waterEffect.Parameters["viewportWidth"].SetValue(
      graphics.Viewport.Width);

    waterEffect.Parameters["viewportHeight"].SetValue(
      graphics.Viewport.Height);
  }
}
```

The first step in the process is to render the scene from the position of a "reflected" camera. Basically, we flip the position and target of the camera across the water's plane and render the area of the scene above the water:

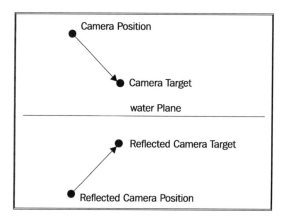

Because the water needs to be able to draw the entire scene at will, we will need to specify a way for it to interact with other objects. All of our classes so far have a common `Draw()` function, so we will simply create an interface with a `Draw()` function that they will all share. Then, the water will be able to tell objects to draw themselves when necessary:

```
public interface IRenderable
{
  void Draw(Matrix View, Matrix Projection, Vector3 CameraPosition);
}
```

Now all we need to do is apply this interface to all of our "renderable" classes:

```
// Make SkySphere IRenderable
public class SkySphere : IRenderable

// Make CModel IRenderable
public class CModel : IRenderable
```

We need two member variables to draw the scene—a list of IRenderables and a render target to render the reflected scene into. Because we want to render our scene from the camera's point of view, we need to keep a few more instance variables—a list of objects to render and a render target to store the rendered scene:

```
RenderTarget2D reflectionTarg;
public List<IRenderable> Objects = new List<IRenderable>();
```

The render target needs to be initialized in the constructor:

```
reflectionTarg = new RenderTarget2D(graphics, graphics.Viewport.Width,
    graphics.Viewport.Height, false, SurfaceFormat.Color,
    DepthFormat.Depth24);
```

As our reflected camera position will be below the water's plane, we want to limit the rendering to only the objects above water. To do so, we will use what is called a **clipping plane**, where we cut off anything below the water's surface when rendering. We'll need to add this functionality to any effect that may intersect our water, so while we will do so only for the sky sphere and cube map reflection effects that we wrote most recently, we would need to do so for any effect to be used in conjunction with the `Water` class.

We will expand our `IRenderable` interface to also require a `SetClipPlane()` function. We represent a clip plane as a `Vector4` with the X, Y, and Z components representing a normal and the final component representing the distance along that normal from the origin:

```
public interface IRenderable
{
```

```
    void Draw(Matrix View, Matrix Projection, Vector3 CameraPosition);
    void SetClipPlane(Vector4? Plane);
}
```

The implementation for the CModel class is simple: if the model's effect supports clip planes, set the clip plane to each effect:

```
public void SetClipPlane(Vector4? Plane)
{
  foreach (ModelMesh mesh in Model.Meshes)
    foreach (ModelMeshPart part in mesh.MeshParts)
    {
      if (part.Effect.Parameters["ClipPlaneEnabled"] != null)
        part.Effect.Parameters["ClipPlaneEnabled"].
          SetValue(Plane.HasValue);

      if (Plane.HasValue)
        if (part.Effect.Parameters["ClipPlane"] != null)
          part.Effect.Parameters["ClipPlane"].SetValue(Plane.Value);
    }
}
```

The implementation for the SkySphere class is even simpler because we know ahead of time what effect parameters the sky effect will have:

```
public void SetClipPlane(Vector4? Plane)
{
  effect.Parameters["ClipPlaneEnabled"].SetValue(Plane.HasValue);

  if (Plane.HasValue)
    effect.Parameters["ClipPlane"].SetValue(Plane.Value);
}
```

We will need to add the relevant effect parameters to any effect that we want to support clip planes, in this case, the CubeMapReflect.fx and skysphere_effect.fx effects:

```
float4 ClipPlane;
bool ClipPlaneEnabled = false;
```

As both of these effects already calculate the world position in the vertex shader, we can simply add the following to the beginning of both of their pixel shaders:

```
if (ClipPlaneEnabled)
  clip(dot(float4(input.WorldPosition, 1), ClipPlane));
```

Now let's get to the effect file. We start with the usual effect paremeters—a texture sampler for the reflected scene render and the view matrix for the reflected camera.

```
float4x4 World;
float4x4 View;
float4x4 Projection;
float3 CameraPosition;
float4x4 ReflectedView;

texture ReflectionMap;

sampler2D reflectionSampler = sampler_state {
    texture = <ReflectionMap>;
    MinFilter = Anisotropic;
    MagFilter = Anisotropic;
};

#include "PPShared.vsi"
```

The vertex shader simply needs to calculate the screen space position of the vertex from the main camera's point of view and from the reflected camera's point of view. We need the latter because it will be used to sample from the reflection map, which is where the reflected view of the scene was rendered.

```
struct VertexShaderInput
{
  float4 Position : POSITION0;
};

struct VertexShaderOutput
{
  float4 Position : POSITION0;
  float4 ReflectionPosition : TEXCOORD1;
};

VertexShaderOutput VertexShaderFunction(VertexShaderInput input)
{
  VertexShaderOutput output;

  float4x4 wvp = mul(World, mul(View, Projection));
  output.Position = mul(input.Position, wvp);

  float4x4 rwvp = mul(World, mul(ReflectedView, Projection));
  output.ReflectionPosition = mul(input.Position, rwvp);

  return output;
}
```

The pixel shader then uses the reflected screen space position of the vertex to sample the reflection from the reflection map. For now, it will just return this value to create a mirror effect.

```
float4 PixelShaderFunction(VertexShaderOutput input) : COLOR0
{
  float2 reflectionUV = postProjToScreen(input.ReflectionPosition) +
    halfPixel();

  float3 reflection = tex2D(reflectionSampler, reflectionUV);

  return float4(reflection, 1);
}
```

Finally, we have our usual technique definition:

```
technique Technique1
{
  pass Pass1
  {
    VertexShader = compile vs_1_1 VertexShaderFunction();
    PixelShader = compile ps_2_0 PixelShaderFunction();
  }
}
```

We can now write a function that will render the scene with the reflected camera, clip planes, and so on into our render target:

```
public void renderReflection(Camera camera)
{
  // Reflect the camera's properties across the water plane
  Vector3 reflectedCameraPosition = ((FreeCamera)camera).Position;
  reflectedCameraPosition.Y = -reflectedCameraPosition.Y +
    waterMesh.Position.Y * 2;

  Vector3 reflectedCameraTarget = ((FreeCamera)camera).Target;
  reflectedCameraTarget.Y = -reflectedCameraTarget.Y
      + waterMesh.Position.Y * 2;

  // Create a temporary camera to render the reflected scene
  Camera reflectionCamera = new TargetCamera(
      reflectedCameraPosition, reflectedCameraTarget, graphics);

  reflectionCamera.Update();

  // Set the reflection camera's view matrix to the water effect
  waterEffect.Parameters["ReflectedView"].SetValue(
    reflectionCamera.View);

  // Create the clip plane
```

```
Vector4 clipPlane = new Vector4(0, 1, 0, -waterMesh.Position.Y);

// Set the render target
graphics.SetRenderTarget(reflectionTarg);
graphics.Clear(Color.Black);

// Draw all objects with clip plane
foreach (IRenderable renderable in Objects)
{
    renderable.SetClipPlane(clipPlane);

    renderable.Draw(reflectionCamera.View, reflectionCamera.Projection,
        reflectedCameraPosition);

    renderable.SetClipPlane(null);
}

graphics.SetRenderTarget(null);

// Set the reflected scene to its effect parameter in
// the water effect
waterEffect.Parameters["ReflectionMap"].SetValue(reflectionTarg);
}
```

We will also add another function to handle the entire pre-drawing process (drawing the scene into the render target):

```
public void PreDraw(Camera camera, GameTime gameTime)
{
    renderReflection(camera);
}
```

Let's see what we have so far by creating a "water effect" in the `Game1` class. First, we need an instance of the class:

```
Water water;
```

We can then initialize this instance in the `LoadContent()` method. Remember that we need to add objects to its list if we want them to be drawn in the reflection:

```
water = new Water(Content, GraphicsDevice,
    new Vector3(0, 0, 0), new Vector2(1000, 1000));

water.Objects.Add(sky);
water.Objects.Add(models[0]);
```

Finally, we need to call its `PreDraw()` and `Draw()` functions in the main `Draw()` function:

```
// Called when the game should draw itself
protected override void Draw(GameTime gameTime)
```

```
{
    water.PreDraw(camera, gameTime);

    GraphicsDevice.Clear(Color.CornflowerBlue);

    sky.Draw(camera.View, camera.Projection, (
        (FreeCamera)camera).Position);
    water.Draw(camera.View, camera.Projection, (
        (FreeCamera)camera).Position);

    foreach (CModel model in models)
        if (camera.BoundingVolumeIsInView(model.BoundingSphere))
            model.Draw(camera.View, camera.Projection,
                ((FreeCamera)camera).Position);

    base.Draw(gameTime);
}
```

Running the game now will show the perfect mirror water effect that we have so far:

You could leave the effect as is if you wanted, for example, a super shiny glass floor. It's not much of a stretch to modify the effect to produce a mirror for other situations, like a mirror on a wall, for example. However, as we are working on a water effect right now, we'll focus on making this look more like water. Let's start by giving it a watery hue. We'll start by adding two new effect parameters:

```
float3 BaseColor = float3(0.2, 0.2, 0.8);
float BaseColorAmount = 0.3f;
```

Now we simply need to blend between the reflection color and the base color in the pixel shader to give it a little tint. The `lerp()` function interpolates between two values by the amount given in the third parameter (0 to 1).

```
return float4(lerp(reflection, BaseColor, BaseColorAmount), 1);
```

This looks a little more like water, but we're missing a huge feature of normal water—*ripples*. We'll simulate water ripples by applying a normal map. However, instead of using it to offset lighting, we're going to use it to modify the sampling position of the reflection map. This will create the illusion that each "wave" is reflecting the scene correctly. The first thing we need is a texture and texture sampler in our shader for the normal map:

```
texture WaterNormalMap;

sampler2D waterNormalSampler = sampler_state {
    texture = <WaterNormalMap>;
};
```

We will also need a few effect parameters that will modify the normal map slightly to adjust the wave size and offset the position over time to make the waves "move" across the surface of the water.

```
float WaveLength = 0.6;
float WaveHeight = 0.2;
float Time = 0;
float WaveSpeed = 0.04f;
```

We'll also need a new value in the `VertexShaderOutput` struct—the position to sample from the normal map. The `VertexShaderInput` struct will need to supply the UV coordinates of the mesh as well:

```
struct VertexShaderInput
{
   float4 Position : POSITION0;
   float2 UV : TEXCOORD0;
};
```

```
struct VertexShaderOutput
{
  float4 Position : POSITION0;
  float4 ReflectionPosition : TEXCOORD1;
  float2 NormalMapPosition : TEXCOORD2;
};
```

The vertex shader, then, will need to calculate this value:

```
output.NormalMapPosition = input.UV/WaveLength;
output.NormalMapPosition.y -= Time * WaveSpeed;
```

Finally, we can modify the pixel shader to use the offset texture coordinates when sampling from the reflection map:

```
float4 normal = tex2D(waterNormalSampler, input.NormalMapPosition) * 2
- 1;
float2 UVOffset = WaveHeight * normal.rg;
float3 reflection = tex2D(reflectionSampler, reflectionUV + UVOffset);
```

Our `WaterEffect` class will need to set the shader parameters that we added for us. At the end of the constructor, add the code to load in the normal map:

```
waterEffect.Parameters["WaterNormalMap"].SetValue(
    content.Load<Texture2D>("water_normal"));
```

At the end of the `PreDraw` method, we will set the `Time` value:

```
waterEffect.Parameters["Time"].SetValue(
    (float)gameTime.TotalGameTime.TotalSeconds);
```

This makes our water ripple like real water:

However, there is a flaw in this image, where the water touches the edge of the screen. Offsetting the UV coordinates that we use to sample from the reflection render target can sometimes result in us using UV coordinates that are past the boundaries of the screen, which by default will be wrapped around to the other side of the texture. This means that at the bottom of the screen, we can actually see the sky where we should see water. To fix this, we can change the "texture address mode" to "mirror", which will reverse the reflected texture when sampled outside of its boundaries. This is not technically correct but it will give the water edges a more correct appearance:

```
sampler2D reflectionSampler = sampler_state {
    texture = <ReflectionMap>;
    MinFilter = Point;
    MagFilter = Point;
    AddressU = Mirror;
    AddressV = Mirror;
};
```

Let's add one finishing touch—specular highlights when the water reflects our light source (in this case, a directional light). We will need one more effect parameter—the light direction.

```
float3 LightDirection = float3(1, 1, 1);
```

Our `VertexShaderOutput` struct will need another value as well:

```
struct VertexShaderOutput
{
    float4 Position : POSITION0;
    float4 ReflectionPosition : TEXCOORD1;
    float2 NormalMapPosition : TEXCOORD2;
    float4 WorldPosition : TEXCOORD3;
};
```

Calculating this value in the vertex shader is easy: we simply multiply the input position by the world matrix:

```
output.WorldPosition = mul(input.Position, World);
```

Finally, we can update the pixel shader to add the specular value to the output. The specular value is calculated the same way as earlier with our model shader:

```
float3 viewDirection = normalize(CameraPosition - input.
WorldPosition);

float3 reflectionVector = -reflect(LightDirection, normal.rgb);
float specular = dot(normalize(reflectionVector), viewDirection);
specular = pow(specular, 256);
return float4(lerp(reflection, BaseColor, BaseColorAmount) + specular,
1);
```

Adding in the specular effect completes our water effect.

Summary

Now that you've reached the end of this chapter, you've seen a number of "shader effects" – special effects that make use of HLSL and the programmable pipeline to get some interesting results that don't have anything to do with lighting per se. You've seen how to implement some extremely simple fog in an effect file, which (as discussed earlier) is both cheap and extremely useful, performance-wise and for dramatic effect.

Next, you saw two ways to use cube maps in a game – mapped to the inside of a sphere placed around the camera to simulate an infinitely far away sky, and mapped to the exterior of a model to implement some relatively cheap non-real-time reflections.

Billboard and Particle Effects

Billboarding is a technique where 2D textures are drawn onto 3D rectangles placed in the scene. In many cases, those rectangles are rotated to face the camera, while in other cases they rotate around a specific axis. We will look at examples of both of these situations to create the effect of 3D clouds and trees. The latter case is interesting because it allows us to efficiently draw huge numbers of trees onto the screen—a number that would be impractical with 3D models. In the following screenshot, the trees and the clouds at the top of the screen are drawn using **billboards**:

From afar, the two methods are often indistinguishable, so many games will do just that: draw 2D "billboards" in place of 3D models until the player gets within a certain distance of an object. Once the player gets close enough that they would see a difference between a billboard and the model, the game will switch to drawing a 3D model instead. This is a common practice in most "level of detail" systems, and so it is a valuable technique to learn. The technique can be used in other ways as well: to simulate more complex objects, such as shrubs or tree leaves, or to draw the muzzle flash for a gun to name a few.

A more advanced use of the billboarding technique is for use in particle effects. **Particles** are just billboards, but they move according to time, fade in and out, change color, and so on to create a variety of effects, such as fire and smoke. We will look at particle systems at the end of this chapter.

Creating the BillboardSystem class

We draw billboards using what are called **vertex buffers** and **index buffers**. A **vertex** is simply a point in 3D space. XNA allows us to specify what information we'd like to store in a vertex, and this information is passed to the vertex shader according to the semantics we specify in the input struct in HLSL. A **vertex buffer** is basically a list of vertices that the graphics card can interact with.

Index buffers help us to cut down on the total number of vertices we have to draw. Instead of using six vertices to describe a rectangle (three vertices per triangle, with two triangles forming a rectangle), we can use four vertices and six indices. An **index buffer** is simply a list of locations (indices) in the vertex buffer that combine to form shapes — triangles in this case. Let's begin by creating a class that will, given the locations of a set of billboards, handle the creation and drawing of those billboards.

```
public class BillboardSystem
{
    // Vertex buffer and index buffer, particle
    // and index arrays
    VertexBuffer verts;
    IndexBuffer ints;
    VertexPositionTexture[] particles;
    int[] indices;

    // Billboard settings
    int nBillboards;
    Vector2 billboardSize;
    Texture2D texture;

    // GraphicsDevice and Effect
    GraphicsDevice graphicsDevice;
    Effect effect;
}
```

Our constructor will need to accept a number of values as well:

```
public BillboardSystem(GraphicsDevice graphicsDevice,
    ContentManager content, Texture2D texture,
    Vector2 billboardSize, Vector3[] particlePositions)
{
  this.nBillboards = particlePositions.Length;
  this.billboardSize = billboardSize;
  this.graphicsDevice = graphicsDevice;
  this.texture = texture;

  effect = content.Load<Effect>("BillboardEffect");
}
```

Our first order of business in the constructor is to initialize the vertex buffers and index buffers. We create four vertices and six indices per billboard. The vertices are all centered at each billboard's location, and are offset later in the vertex shader based on their texture coordinates. The six indices allow us to create two triangles from four vertices:

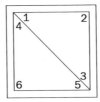

```
void generateParticles(Vector3[] particlePositions)
{
  // Create vertex and index arrays
  particles = new VertexPositionTexture[nBillboards * 4];
  indices = new int[nBillboards * 6];

  int x = 0;

  // For each billboard...
  for (int i = 0; i < nBillboards * 4; i += 4)
  {
    Vector3 pos = particlePositions[i / 4];

    // Add 4 vertices at the billboard's position
    particles[i + 0] = new VertexPositionTexture(pos,
      new Vector2(0, 0));
    particles[i + 1] = new VertexPositionTexture(pos,
      new Vector2(0, 1));
```

```
    particles[i + 2] = new VertexPositionTexture(pos,
        new Vector2(1, 1));
    particles[i + 3] = new VertexPositionTexture(pos,
        new Vector2(1, 0));

    // Add 6 indices to form two triangles
    indices[x++] = i + 0;
    indices[x++] = i + 3;
    indices[x++] = i + 2;
    indices[x++] = i + 2;
    indices[x++] = i + 1;
    indices[x++] = i + 0;
}


// Create and set the vertex buffer
verts = new VertexBuffer(graphicsDevice,
    typeof(VertexPositionTexture),
    nBillboards * 4, BufferUsage.WriteOnly);
verts.SetData<VertexPositionTexture>(particles);

// Create and set the index buffer
ints = new IndexBuffer(graphicsDevice,
    IndexElementSize.ThirtyTwoBits,
    nBillboards * 6, BufferUsage.WriteOnly);
ints.SetData<int>(indices);
}
```

We need to call this function at the end of the constructor:

```
generateParticles(particlePositions);
```

As noted earlier, there are four vertices for each billboard. However, note that we are not actually placing a vertex at each corner of the billboard as you may expect, but are instead placing all six vertices at the billboard's position. At this point, the vertices are not offset from the billboard position at all but are clustered around the same point. Instead, we are storing the corner of the billboard at which each vertex is positioned into the texture coordinate data.

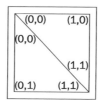

In this way, we can offset the positions of the vertex on the GPU rather than on the CPU. This will speed up our rendering significantly because we will not need to update every billboard, every frame on the CPU and then spend time updating the vertex buffer—instead, almost all of the work will be done by the GPU.

Drawing Billboards

With our vertex and index buffers set up, we are ready to write the code that draws our billboards. First, we will need a function to set all of our `effect` parameters to our soon-to-be-written effect:

```
void setEffectParameters(Matrix View, Matrix Projection, Vector3 Up,
  Vector3 Right)
{
  effect.Parameters["ParticleTexture"].SetValue(texture);
  effect.Parameters["View"].SetValue(View);
  effect.Parameters["Projection"].SetValue(Projection);
  effect.Parameters["Size"].SetValue(billboardSize / 2f);
  effect.Parameters["Up"].SetValue(Up);
  effect.Parameters["Side"].SetValue(Right);

  effect.CurrentTechnique.Passes[0].Apply();
}
```

The `Up` and `Right` vectors are especially important, as these are the axes along which we will move the vertices from their center position based on their texture coordinates:

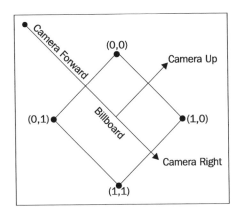

We can now write the `Draw()` function:

```
public void Draw(Matrix View, Matrix Projection, Vector3 Up, Vector3
Right)
{
  // Set the vertex and index buffer to the graphics card
  graphicsDevice.SetVertexBuffer(verts);
  graphicsDevice.Indices = ints;

  setEffectParameters(View, Projection, Up, Right);

  // Draw the billboards
    graphicsDevice.DrawIndexedPrimitives(PrimitiveType.TriangleList,
        0, 0, 4 * nBillboards, 0, nBillboards * 2);

  // Un-set the vertex and index buffer
  graphicsDevice.SetVertexBuffer(null);
  graphicsDevice.Indices = null;
}
```

We can also write the HLSL effect. Add a new effect called `BillboardEffect.fx`. The effect will have parameters that reflect those listed earlier:

```
float4x4 View;
float4x4 Projection;

texture ParticleTexture;
sampler2D texSampler = sampler_state {
   texture = <ParticleTexture>;
};

float2 Size;
float3 Up; // Camera's 'up' vector
float3 Side; // Camera's 'side' vector
```

As we are using the `VertexPositionTexture` vertex type, the only values the vertex shader needs to receive and return are the position and UV coordinates of each vertex:

```
struct VertexShaderInput
{
  float4 Position : POSITION0;
  float2 UV : TEXCOORD0;
};
```

```
struct VertexShaderOutput
{
  float4 Position : POSITION0;
  float2 UV : TEXCOORD0;
};
```

The vertex shader then transforms the vertex's position to the corner of the rectangle it represents based on its UV coordinates:

```
VertexShaderOutput VertexShaderFunction(VertexShaderInput input)
{
  VertexShaderOutput output;

  float3 position = input.Position;

  // Determine which corner of the rectangle this vertex
  // represents
  float2 offset = float2((input.UV.x - 0.5f) * 2.0f,
      -(input.UV.y - 0.5f) * 2.0f);

  // Move the vertex along the camera's 'plane' to its corner
  position += offset.x * Size.x * Side + offset.y * Size.y * Up;

  // Transform the position by view and projection
  output.Position = mul(float4(position, 1), mul(View, Projection));

  output.UV = input.UV;

  return output;
}
```

Finally, the pixel shader simply samples the texture and returns the value. The technique definition is very standard as well:

```
float4 PixelShaderFunction(VertexShaderOutput input) : COLOR0
{
  float4 color = tex2D(texSampler, input.UV);

  return color;
}

technique Technique1
{
  pass Pass1
  {
    VertexShader = compile vs_2_0 VertexShaderFunction();
```

```
        PixelShader = compile ps_2_0 PixelShaderFunction();
    }
}
```

Let's create an instance of the `BillboardSystem` class in our `Game1` class to see how it looks:

```
BillboardSystem trees;
```

We'll need to initialize it in the constructor:

```
// Generate random tree positions
Random r = new Random();
Vector3[] positions = new Vector3[100];

for (int i = 0; i < positions.Length; i++)
    positions[i] = new Vector3((float)r.NextDouble() * 20000 - 10000,
        400, (float)r.NextDouble() * 20000 - 10000);

trees = new BillboardSystem(GraphicsDevice, Content,
    Content.Load<Texture2D>("tree_billboard"), new Vector2(800),
positions);
```

Note that we'll need access to the vectors pointing up and to the right from the camera's point of view. For brevity's sake we'll just make these public properties of the `FreeCamera` class:

```
public Vector3 Up { get; private set; }
public Vector3 Right { get; private set; }
```

These values can then be set at the end of the `Update()` function of the `FreeCamera` class:

```
this.Up = up;
this.Right = Vector3.Cross(forward, up);
```

Finally, we need to make sure to call the `Draw()` method of the `BillboardSystem` class in the game's `Draw()` method, after the models have been drawn:

```
trees.Draw(camera.View, camera.Projection, ((FreeCamera)camera).Up,
    ((FreeCamera)camera).Right);
```

Drawing this way will indeed draw all of the polygons to the screen, but right off the bat there is a problem: our billboards are not being drawn with transparency.

As this billboard texture has an **alpha channel** (transparency), we would expect it to blend in with the scene. To fix this, we need to enable **alpha blending** before drawing the polygons:

```
// Enable alpha blending
graphicsDevice.BlendState = BlendState.AlphaBlend;

// Draw the billboards
graphicsDevice.DrawIndexedPrimitives(PrimitiveType.TriangleList, 0, 0,
    4 * nBillboards, 0, nBillboards * 2);

// Reset render states
graphicsDevice.BlendState = BlendState.Opaque;
```

Enabling transparency, however, creates a second, more subtle problem: our billboards are obscuring each other, despite being drawn transparently. This is because the **depth buffer** is still being used to determine which polygons are obscuring other polygons.

We could solve this problem by disabling the depth buffer when drawing our billboards, but then we would end up with yet another issue where billboards drawn later would obscure other billboards, even if the latter billboards are closer to the camera:

This is a somewhat complex problem with two solutions. The first solution would be to sort all of the billboards from back to front when drawing, so that the closer billboards would always be drawn on top of the farther billboards. This would be the most accurate way to solve the problem, but it would also be incredibly inefficient: sorting potentially hundreds of billboards by their distance from the camera would take a long time, especially considering that this technique is meant to save time.

Luckily, there is a simpler solution: instead of drawing all the billboards in one pass, we will draw all of them twice but will draw only certain parts of them each time. In the first pass, we will draw those sections that are completely or mostly opaque—in other words, we will draw the "solid" parts of the billboard first. During the first pass, we will allow our billboards to write to the depth buffer so that these solid areas will obscure other billboards. We first need to update our effect to discard pixels below a certain transparency threshold:

```
bool AlphaTest = true;
float AlphaTestValue = 0.5f;
```

In the pixel shader, we will use the `clip()` function again to discard pixels below the `AlphaTestValue` parameter:

```
float4 PixelShaderFunction(VertexShaderOutput input) : COLOR0
{
    float4 color = tex2D(texSampler, input.UV);

    if (AlphaTest)
```

```
            clip((color.a - AlphaTestValue) * (AlphaTestGreater ? 1 : -1));

      return color;
   }
```

Back in the `BillboardSystem` class, we will add a function to draw the opaque parts of our billboards:

```
   void drawOpaquePixels()
   {
      graphicsDevice.DepthStencilState = DepthStencilState.Default;

      effect.Parameters["AlphaTest"].SetValue(true);
      effect.Parameters["AlphaTestGreater"].SetValue(true);

      drawBillboards();
   }

   void drawBillboards()
   {
      effect.CurrentTechnique.Passes[0].Apply();

      graphicsDevice.DrawIndexedPrimitives(PrimitiveType.TriangleList, 0, 0,
          4 * nBillboards, 0, nBillboards * 2);
   }
```

During the second pass, we will draw only the transparent parts of each billboard, but this time we will do so with the depth buffer disabled. In this way, the sections being drawn will still be obscured by other billboards, but will not obscure billboards drawn after them. While this is not always technically correct, as some transparent parts of billboards may be drawn over the transparent parts of billboards drawn before them, the effect is usually not noticeable.

```
   void drawTransparentPixels()
   {
      graphicsDevice.DepthStencilState = DepthStencilState.DepthRead;

      effect.Parameters["AlphaTest"].SetValue(true);
      effect.Parameters["AlphaTestGreater"].SetValue(false);

      drawBillboards();
   }
```

The last step is to update the `Draw()` method to use these two functions. However, we should probably give the user the option to choose which method of drawing to use: simple drawing or occlusion-ensured drawing. In this way, if the user is drawing a large number of mostly transparent billboards, where most of the pixels will be drawn without occlusion anyway (clouds, for example), they will not waste time drawing everything twice:

```
public bool EnsureOcclusion = true;
```

We then check this value in the `Draw()` method:

```
public void Draw(Matrix View, Matrix Projection, Vector3 Up, Vector3
Right)
{
  // Set the vertex and index buffer to the graphics card
  graphicsDevice.SetVertexBuffer(verts);
  graphicsDevice.Indices = ints;

  graphicsDevice.BlendState = BlendState.AlphaBlend;

  setEffectParameters(View, Projection, Up, Right);

  if (EnsureOcclusion)
  {
    drawOpaquePixels();
    drawTransparentPixels();
  }
  else
  {
    graphicsDevice.DepthStencilState = DepthStencilState.DepthRead;
    effect.Parameters["AlphaTest"].SetValue(false);
    drawBillboards();
  }

  // Reset render states
  graphicsDevice.BlendState = BlendState.Opaque;
  graphicsDevice.DepthStencilState = DepthStencilState.Default;

  // Un-set the vertex and index buffer
  graphicsDevice.SetVertexBuffer(null);
  graphicsDevice.Indices = null;
}
```

If we run the game now, we can see that the trees are all rendering nicely, from any horizontal angle:

There is, however, one final problem. If we look at the scene from the previous screenshot, the trees will continue to rotate to face the camera. This works for some billboards (clouds, smoke particles, and so on) but does not work very well for objects that are trying to approximate 3D objects, such as trees that are rooted in one spot:

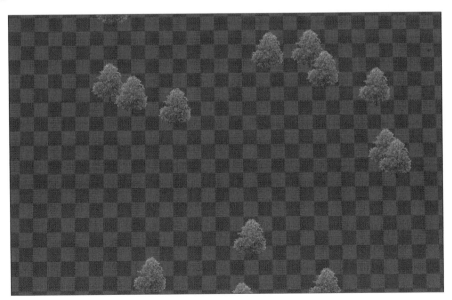

What we are currently doing is called spherical billboarding. With **spherical billboarding**, billboards will turn to face the camera no matter what angle the camera is viewing them from. To solve this problem we will switch to **cylindrical billboarding**, which will limit rotation to the Y axis. However, we want to allow the user to switch between the two modes depending on the desired effect:

```
public enum BillboardMode { Cylindrical, Spherical };
public BillboardMode Mode = BillboardMode.Spherical;
```

To change which mode we are using we simply switch between using the camera's "up" vector or the literal "up" vector (0, 1, 0) in the setEffectParameters() method:

```
effect.Parameters["Up"].SetValue(Mode == BillboardMode.Spherical ?
  Up : Vector3.Up);
```

Switching to cylindrical billboarding in the game's class will give us the desired result:

```
trees.Mode = BillboardSystem.BillboardMode.Cylindrical;
```

Creating clouds with spherical billboarding

Now that our BillboardSystem class is complete, let's add another instance of it to the Game1 class using the opposite Mode and EnsureOcclusion settings to draw clouds:

```
BillboardSystem clouds;
```

We'll need to initialize this like our trees instance:

```
Vector3[] cloudPositions = new Vector3[350];

for (int i = 0; i < cloudPositions.Length; i++)
{
```

```
    cloudPositions[i] = new Vector3(
        r.Next(-6000, 6000),
        r.Next(2000, 3000),
        r.Next(-6000, 6000));
}

clouds = new BillboardSystem(GraphicsDevice, Content,
    Content.Load<Texture2D>("cloud2"), new Vector2(1000),
    cloudPositions);

clouds.EnsureOcclusion = false;
```

Non-rotating billboards

Another way to use billboards is to simply place them in 3D space and leave them as is. This is useful to approximate various shapes without having them rotate all the time — a bush or shrub, for example. This is more practical for up-close drawing because they still look as complex as a model, but don't require a model to be drawn containing hundreds of vertices:

In this style of billboarding, we build a "cross" out of two rectangles that will simulate a 3D object:

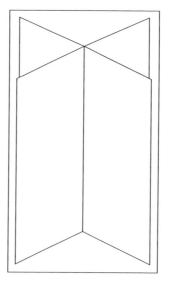

The class that handles this is very similar to the `BillboardSystem` class, but makes a few simplifying changes, and has some changes when creating vertices and indices. Begin by copying the `BillboardSystem` class, and rename it to `BillboardCross`. You will need to change the classname and reflect that change in the constructor. You can then remove the `Mode` enumeration and member variable. The differences arise first in the `generateParticles()` function, where we create two rectangles per billboard instead of one. Note that we are also placing vertices directly in 3D space rather than transforming them in a shader:

```
void generateParticles(Vector3[] particlePositions)
{
    // Create vertex and index arrays
    particles = new VertexPositionTexture[nBillboards * 8];
    indices = new int[nBillboards * 12];

    int x = 0;

    // For each billboard...
    for (int i = 0; i < nBillboards * 8; i += 8)
    {
```

```
    Vector3 pos = particlePositions[i / 8];

    Vector3 offsetX = new Vector3(billboardSize.X/2.0f,
     billboardSize.Y/2.0f, 0);
    Vector3 offsetZ = new Vector3(0, offsetX.Y, offsetX.X);

    // Add 4 vertices per rectangle
    particles[i + 0] = new VertexPositionTexture(pos +
     new Vector3(-1, 1, 0) * offsetX, new Vector2(0, 0));
    particles[i + 1] = new VertexPositionTexture(pos +
     new Vector3(-1, -1, 0) * offsetX, new Vector2(0, 1));
    particles[i + 2] = new VertexPositionTexture(pos +
     new Vector3(1, -1, 0) * offsetX, new Vector2(1, 1));
    particles[i + 3] = new VertexPositionTexture(pos +
     new Vector3(1, 1, 0) * offsetX, new Vector2(1, 0));

    particles[i + 4] = new VertexPositionTexture(pos +
     new Vector3(0, 1, -1) * offsetZ, new Vector2(0, 0));
    particles[i + 5] = new VertexPositionTexture(pos +
     new Vector3(0, -1, -1) * offsetZ, new Vector2(0, 1));
    particles[i + 6] = new VertexPositionTexture(pos +
     new Vector3(0, -1, 1) * offsetZ, new Vector2(1, 1));
    particles[i + 7] = new VertexPositionTexture(pos +
     new Vector3(0, 1, 1) * offsetZ, new Vector2(1, 0));

    // Add 6 indices per rectangle to form four triangles
    indices[x++] = i + 0;
    indices[x++] = i + 3;
    indices[x++] = i + 2;
    indices[x++] = i + 2;
    indices[x++] = i + 1;
    indices[x++] = i + 0;

    indices[x++] = i + 0 + 4;
    indices[x++] = i + 3 + 4;
    indices[x++] = i + 2 + 4;
    indices[x++] = i + 2 + 4;
    indices[x++] = i + 1 + 4;
    indices[x++] = i + 0 + 4;
}
```

```
    // Create and set the vertex buffer
    verts = new VertexBuffer(graphicsDevice,
        typeof(VertexPositionTexture),
        nBillboards * 8, BufferUsage.WriteOnly);
    verts.SetData<VertexPositionTexture>(particles);

    // Create and set the index buffer
    ints = new IndexBuffer(graphicsDevice,
        IndexElementSize.ThirtyTwoBits,
        nBillboards * 12, BufferUsage.WriteOnly);
    ints.SetData<int>(indices);
}
```

The only other difference is in the drawBillboards() function where we must draw
twice as many triangles:

```
void drawBillboards()
{
  effect.CurrentTechnique.Passes[0].Apply();

  graphicsDevice.DrawIndexedPrimitives(PrimitiveType.TriangleList, 0,
  0, nBillboards * 8, 0, nBillboards * 4);
}
```

The effect is also a duplicate of the BillboardEffect.fx effect, save for a few
simplifying changes. First, we will no longer need the Up or Side parameters.
Second, the vertex shader will only need to transform our vertices' positions
with the view and projection matrices:

```
VertexShaderOutput VertexShaderFunction(VertexShaderInput input)
{
  VertexShaderOutput output;

  output.Position = mul(input.Position, mul(View, Projection));
  output.UV = input.UV;

  return output;
}
```

Back in the `BillboardCross` class, the `setEffectParameters()` function will no longer need to set the `Side` or `Up` parameters. Additionally, we will no longer need to pass those parameters to the `setEffectParameters()` or `Draw()` functions, so you may remove them:

```
void setEffectParameters(Matrix View, Matrix Projection)
{
   effect.Parameters["ParticleTexture"].SetValue(texture);
   effect.Parameters["View"].SetValue(View);
   effect.Parameters["Projection"].SetValue(Projection);
}
```

Finally, we need to switch to the new `effect` in the constructor:

```
effect = content.Load<Effect>("BillboardCrossEffect");
```

To use this new system in our game, we can switch the `trees` member variable to a `BillboardCross` variable:

```
BillboardCross trees;
```

We initialize this using the same random positions but with slightly different arguments:

```
trees = new BillboardCross(GraphicsDevice, Content,
      Content.Load<Texture2D>("tree_billboard"), new Vector2(800),
   positions);
```

Finally, our `Draw()` call must be changed so as not to pass the `Right` or `Up` parameters:

```
trees.Draw(camera.View, camera.Projection);
```

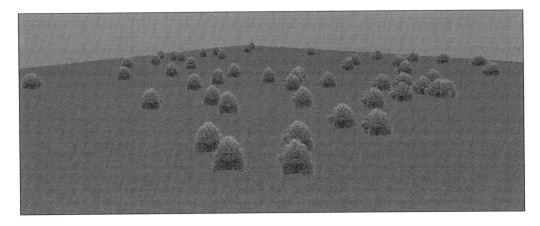

Particle effects

The final topic we are going to look at is particle effects. **Particles** are basically billboards, but in addition to being rotated to face the camera we move them over time. For example, we may specify a starting position, direction, and speed, and move each particle along its direction at its speed from its starting position based on the time that has elapsed since the particle began moving in the vertex shader. It is possible to create very complicated effects using particles, as they are relatively cheap—fire, smoke, and so on, are all easily achieved and convincing using particle systems.

In this case, we will specify a starting position, movement direction, speed, lifetime, fade in time, and "wind" value (which moves all particles uniformly in a given direction over time) for our particles. Because we want to specify all of these specific values per particle we will need a custom **vertex format**:

```
struct ParticleVertex : IVertexType
{
  Vector3 startPosition;
  Vector2 uv;
  Vector3 direction;
  float speed;
  float startTime;

  // Starting position of that particle (t = 0)
  public Vector3 StartPosition
  {
     get { return startPosition; }
     set { startPosition = value; }
  }

  // UV coordinate, used for texturing and to offset vertex in shader
  public Vector2 UV
  {
     get { return uv; }
     set { uv = value; }
  }

  // Movement direction of the particle
  public Vector3 Direction
  {
    get { return direction; }
    set { direction = value; }
  }
```

```csharp
// Speed of the particle in units/second
public float Speed
{
    get { return speed; }
    set { speed = value; }
}


// The time since the particle system was created that this
// particle came into use
public float StartTime
{
    get { return startTime; }
    set { startTime = value; }
}

public ParticleVertex(Vector3 StartPosition, Vector2 UV,
 Vector3 Direction, float Speed, float StartTime)
{
    this.startPosition = StartPosition;
    this.uv = UV;
    this.direction = Direction;
    this.speed = Speed;
    this.startTime = StartTime;
}


// Vertex declaration
public readonly static VertexDeclaration VertexDeclaration =
    new VertexDeclaration(
    new VertexElement(0, VertexElementFormat.Vector3,
        // Start position
         VertexElementUsage.Position, 0),
    new VertexElement(12, VertexElementFormat.Vector2,
        // UV coordinates
         VertexElementUsage.TextureCoordinate, 0),
    new VertexElement(20, VertexElementFormat.Vector3,
        // Movement direction
         VertexElementUsage.TextureCoordinate, 1),
    new VertexElement(32, VertexElementFormat.Single,
        // Movement speed
         VertexElementUsage.TextureCoordinate, 2),
    new VertexElement(36, VertexElementFormat.Single,
        // Start time
         VertexElementUsage.TextureCoordinate, 3)
    );

  VertexDeclaration IVertexType.VertexDeclaration {
    get { return VertexDeclaration; } }
}
```

This format will allow us to create vertices with the information we need to render them properly. That data is passed to the vertex shader through the vertex shader input struct's properties and their corresponding semantics, where we will use them to determine the vertex's final position.

The major difference between the two billboarding systems we have created thus far and a particle system is that a particle system recycles used particles when they reach the end of their life span. We use what is called a **circular queue** to reclaim and reuse particles that have lived long enough to have faded out. This is especially easy because, in this particle system, all particles will have the same life span. We keep track of two variables marking the start and end indices of the particles that are currently "active" (visible), move the start index forward as particles expire, and move the end index forward as new particles are added:

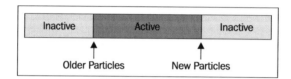

We will need a number of familiar instance variables and the variables mentioned earlier:

```
public class ParticleSystem
{
  // Vertex and index buffers
  VertexBuffer verts;
  IndexBuffer ints;

  // Graphics device and effect
  GraphicsDevice graphicsDevice;
  Effect effect;

  // Particle settings
  int nParticles;
  Vector2 particleSize;
  float lifespan = 1;
  Vector3 wind;
  Texture2D texture;
  float fadeInTime;

  // Particles and indices
  ParticleVertex[] particles;
  int[] indices;
```

```
   // Queue variables
   int activeStart = 0, nActive = 0;

   // Time particle system was created
   DateTime start;
}
```

The constructor and generateParticles() functions may also appear familiar:

```
public ParticleSystem(GraphicsDevice graphicsDevice,
    ContentManager content, Texture2D tex, int nParticles,
    Vector2 particleSize, float lifespan,
    Vector3 wind, float FadeInTime)
{
  this.nParticles = nParticles;
  this.particleSize = particleSize;
  this.lifespan = lifespan;
  this.graphicsDevice = graphicsDevice;
  this.wind = wind;
  this.texture = tex;
  this.fadeInTime = FadeInTime;

  // Create vertex and index buffers to accomodate all particles
  verts = new VertexBuffer(graphicsDevice, typeof(ParticleVertex),
      nParticles * 4, BufferUsage.WriteOnly);

  ints = new IndexBuffer(graphicsDevice,
          IndexElementSize.ThirtyTwoBits, nParticles * 6,
          BufferUsage.WriteOnly);

  generateParticles();

  effect = content.Load<Effect>("ParticleEffect");

  start = DateTime.Now;
}

void generateParticles()
{
  // Create particle and index arrays
  particles = new ParticleVertex[nParticles * 4];
  indices = new int[nParticles * 6];

  Vector3 z = Vector3.Zero;
```

```
            int x = 0;

            // Initialize particle settings and fill index and vertex arrays
            for (int i = 0; i < nParticles * 4; i += 4)
            {
                particles[i + 0] = new ParticleVertex(z, new Vector2(0, 0),
                                        z, 0, -1);
                particles[i + 1] = new ParticleVertex(z, new Vector2(0, 1),
                                        z, 0, -1);
                particles[i + 2] = new ParticleVertex(z, new Vector2(1, 1),
                                        z, 0, -1);
                particles[i + 3] = new ParticleVertex(z, new Vector2(1, 0),
                                        z, 0, -1);

                indices[x++] = i + 0;
                indices[x++] = i + 3;
                indices[x++] = i + 2;
                indices[x++] = i + 2;
                indices[x++] = i + 1;
                indices[x++] = i + 0;
            }
        }
```

The `AddParticle()` function is where things get interesting. We first check if there is enough room in the queue to bring another particle to life, and if so, we do it by applying the particle settings we are giving to the particle:

```
        // Marks another particle as active and applies the given settings to
        it
        public void AddParticle(Vector3 Position, Vector3 Direction, float
        Speed)
        {
            // If there are no available particles, give up
            if (nActive + 4 == nParticles * 4)
                return;

            // Determine the index at which this particle should be created
            int index = offsetIndex(activeStart, nActive);
            nActive += 4;

            // Determine the start time
            float startTime = (float)(DateTime.Now - start).TotalSeconds;

            // Set the particle settings to each of the particle's vertices
            for (int i = 0; i < 4; i++)
```

```
    {
        particles[index + i].StartPosition = Position;
        particles[index + i].Direction = Direction;
        particles[index + i].Speed = Speed;
        particles[index + i].StartTime = startTime;
    }
}

// Increases the 'start' parameter by 'count' positions, wrapping
// around the particle array if necessary
int offsetIndex(int start, int count)
{
    for (int i = 0; i < count; i++)
    {
        start++;

        if (start == particles.Length)
            start = 0;
    }

    return start;
}
```

The Update() function goes through the list of active particles and marks them as inactive if they have aged past the lifetime. Finally, it updates the vertex and index buffers. In a more complex implementation, we could specify that those buffers contain only the active particles to reduce overhead, but for simplicity's sake, we will simply update the entirety of the two buffers.

```
public void Update()
{
    float now = (float)(DateTime.Now - start).TotalSeconds;

    int startIndex = activeStart;
    int end = nActive;

    // For each particle marked as active...
    for (int i = 0; i < end; i++)
    {
        // If this particle has gotten older than 'lifespan'...
        if (particles[activeStart].StartTime < now - lifespan)
        {
            // Advance the active particle start position past
            // the particle's index and reduce the number of
            // active particles by 1
```

```
                activeStart++;
                nActive--;

                if (activeStart == particles.Length)
                  activeStart = 0;
            }
        }


        // Update the vertex and index buffers
        verts.SetData<ParticleVertex>(particles);
        ints.SetData<int>(indices);
    }
```

The Draw() function is also similar to those in our previous two classes, simply drawing all of the particles with various blending states and our effect applied:

```
public void Draw(Matrix View, Matrix Projection, Vector3 Up, Vector3 Right)
{
    // Set the vertex and index buffer to the graphics card
    graphicsDevice.SetVertexBuffer(verts);
    graphicsDevice.Indices = ints;

    // Set the effect parameters
    effect.Parameters["ParticleTexture"].SetValue(texture);
    effect.Parameters["View"].SetValue(View);
    effect.Parameters["Projection"].SetValue(Projection);
    effect.Parameters["Time"].SetValue((float)(DateTime.Now - start).
            TotalSeconds);
    effect.Parameters["Lifespan"].SetValue(lifespan);
    effect.Parameters["Wind"].SetValue(wind);
    effect.Parameters["Size"].SetValue(particleSize / 2f);
    effect.Parameters["Up"].SetValue(Up);
    effect.Parameters["Side"].SetValue(Right);
    effect.Parameters["FadeInTime"].SetValue(fadeInTime);

    // Enable blending render states
    graphicsDevice.BlendState = BlendState.AlphaBlend;
    graphicsDevice.DepthStencilState = DepthStencilState.DepthRead;

    // Apply the effect
    effect.CurrentTechnique.Passes[0].Apply();
```

```
  // Draw the billboards
  graphicsDevice.DrawIndexedPrimitives(PrimitiveType.TriangleList,
    0, 0, nParticles * 4, 0, nParticles * 2);

  // Un-set the buffers
  graphicsDevice.SetVertexBuffer(null);
  graphicsDevice.Indices = null;

  // Reset render states
  graphicsDevice.BlendState = BlendState.Opaque;
  graphicsDevice.DepthStencilState = DepthStencilState.Default;
}
```

Now that the `ParticleSystem` class has been written, we can write the effect (`ParticleEffect.fx`). The `effect` parameters mirror those that are set in the `Draw()` function:

```
float4x4 View;
float4x4 Projection;

texture ParticleTexture;
sampler2D texSampler = sampler_state {
   texture = <ParticleTexture>;
};

float Time;
float Lifespan;
float2 Size;
float3 Wind;
float3 Up;
float3 Side;
float FadeInTime;
```

The `VertexShaderInput` struct matches the values of our custom vertex format:

```
struct VertexShaderInput
{
  float4 Position : POSITION0;
  float2 UV : TEXCOORD0;
  float3 Direction : TEXCOORD1;
  float Speed :  TEXCOORD2;
  float StartTime : TEXCOORD3;
};
```

The role of the vertex shader, then, will be to calculate the final position of each vertex (including moving them to their respective billboard corners). Additionally, the vertex shader will pass through the texture coordinates and will determine the total length of time that the current particle has been active:

```
struct VertexShaderOutput
{
    float4 Position : POSITION0;
    float2 UV : TEXCOORD0;
    float2 RelativeTime : TEXCOORD1;
};


VertexShaderOutput VertexShaderFunction(VertexShaderInput input)
{
    VertexShaderOutput output;

    float3 position = input.Position;

    // Move to billboard corner
    float2 offset = Size * float2((input.UV.x - 0.5f) * 2.0f,
        -(input.UV.y - 0.5f) * 2.0f);
    position += offset.x * Side + offset.y * Up;

    // Determine how long this particle has been alive
    float relativeTime = (Time - input.StartTime);
    output.RelativeTime = relativeTime;

    // Move the vertex along its movement direction and the wind
direction
    position += (input.Direction * input.Speed + Wind) * relativeTime;

    // Transform the final position by the view and projection matrices
    output.Position = mul(float4(position, 1), mul(View, Projection));

    output.UV = input.UV;

    return output;
}
```

The pixel shader fades the particle in and out based on how close to the start and end of its life it is:

```
float4 PixelShaderFunction(VertexShaderOutput input) : COLOR0
{
    // Ignore particles that aren't active
    clip(input.RelativeTime);

    // Sample texture
    float4 color = tex2D(texSampler, input.UV);

    // Fade out towards end of life
    float d = clamp(1.0f - pow((input.RelativeTime / Lifespan), 10),
            0, 1);

    // Fade in at beginning of life
    d *= clamp((input.RelativeTime / FadeInTime), 0, 1);

    // Return color * fade amount
    return float4(color * d);
}
```

The technique definition is similar to those we have been using:

```
technique Technique1
{
  pass Pass1
  {
    VertexShader = compile vs_2_0 VertexShaderFunction();
    PixelShader = compile ps_2_0 PixelShaderFunction();
  }
}
```

Particle fire

The first effect we will create with our particle system is a "fire" effect. To start, we will need an instance of the `ParticleSystem` class. We will also need a random number generator:

```
ParticleSystem ps;
Random r = new Random();
```

We initialize the particle system using the following settings:

```
ps = new ParticleSystem(GraphicsDevice, Content, Content.Load<Texture
2D>("fire"),
    400, new Vector2(400), 1, Vector3.Zero, 0.5f);
```

Every frame, we will add a "new" particle to the particle system at a random position within 400 units of the origin, a direction within 15 degrees of the "up" vector (0, 1, 0), and a random speed between 600 and 900 units per second:

```
// Called when the game should update itself
protected override void Update(GameTime gameTime)
{
   updateCamera(gameTime);

   // Generate a direction within 15 degrees of (0, 1, 0)
   Vector3 offset = new Vector3(MathHelper.ToRadians(10.0f));
   Vector3 randAngle = Vector3.Up + randVec3(-offset, offset);

   // Generate a position between (-400, 0, -400) and (400, 0, 400)
   Vector3 randPosition = randVec3(new Vector3(-400), new
Vector3(400));

   // Generate a speed between 600 and 900
   float randSpeed = (float)r.NextDouble() * 300 + 600;

   ps.AddParticle(randPosition, randAngle, randSpeed);
   ps.Update();

   base.Update(gameTime);
}

// Returns a random Vector3 between min and max
Vector3 randVec3(Vector3 min, Vector3 max)
{
   return new Vector3(
      min.X + (float)r.NextDouble() * (max.X - min.X),
      min.Y + (float)r.NextDouble() * (max.Y - min.Y),
      min.Z + (float)r.NextDouble() * (max.Z - min.Z));
}
```

Finally, we need to draw our particle system in the `Draw()` function after the models have been drawn:

```
ps.Draw(camera.View, camera.Projection,
    ((FreeCamera)camera).Up, ((FreeCamera)camera).Right);
```

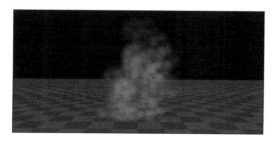

Particle smoke

As our last example, let's add some smoke to our fire effect. We'll need a second `ParticleSystem`:

```
ParticleSystem smoke;
```

We will initialize this particle system the same way, except this time we will use a longer lifetime and fade in time, and we will make use of the "wind" parameter:

```
smoke = new ParticleSystem(GraphicsDevice, Content,
    Content.Load<Texture2D>("smoke"), 400, new Vector2(800), 6,
    new Vector3(500, 0, 0), 5f);
```

For convenience's sake, we will reuse the random values that we have generated when adding the particle and will simply offset the start position on the Y axis:

```
smoke.AddParticle(randPosition + new Vector3(0, 1200, 0), randAngle,
randSpeed);
smoke.Update();
```

Finally, we draw it the same way we drew our fire particles:

```
smoke.Draw(camera.View, camera.Projection,
    ((FreeCamera)camera).Up, ((FreeCamera)camera).Right);
```

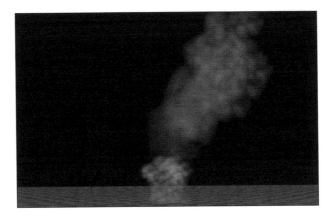

Summary

Having finished this chapter, you've seen a number of different uses and implementations of billboarding effects. You've seen how to do basic spherical and cylindrical billboarding to "fake" 3D objects or create volumetric effects, such as clouds. You've also seen how to create billboards out of vertices that do not turn to face the camera to better fake 3D objects, especially foliage.

Finally, you learned how to implement a somewhat basic particle system and learned how to create fire and smoke effects with it. The particle system is extensible enough that you should be able to build off of it and create new effects in the future. In the next chapter, we will combine these systems with those created in previous chapters to create a rather impressive 3D environment complete with foliage, terrain, clouds, a sky box, and water.

7
Environmental Effects

In this chapter, we will focus on building a full 3D environment. We will start by creating a class that builds a terrain from a 2D image called a **heightmap**. We will make a number of improvements to the basic version of this class, allowing multiple textures across its surface through **multitexturing** and extra detail at close distances to its surface through a "detail texture". We will look at a technique called **region growing** to add plants and trees to the terrain's surface, and finish by combining the terrain with our sky box, water, and billboarding effects to create a mountain scene:

Building a terrain from a heightmap

A **heightmap** is a 2D image that stores, in each pixel, the height of the corresponding point on a grid of vertices. The pixel values range from 0 to 1, so in practice we will multiply them by the maximum height of the terrain to get the final height of each vertex. We build a terrain out of vertices and indices as a large rectangular grid with the same number of vertices as the number of pixels in the heightmap.

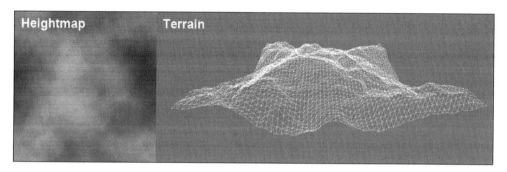

Let's start by creating a new `Terrain` class. This class will keep track of everything needed to render our terrain: textures, the effect, vertex and index buffers, and so on.

```
public class Terrain
{
    VertexPositionNormalTexture[] vertices; // Vertex array
    VertexBuffer vertexBuffer; // Vertex buffer
    int[] indices; // Index array
    IndexBuffer indexBuffer; // Index buffer
    float[,] heights; // Array of vertex heights
    float height; // Maximum height of terrain
    float cellSize; // Distance between vertices on x and z axes
    int width, length; // Number of vertices on x and z axes
    int nVertices, nIndices; // Number of vertices and indices
    Effect effect; // Effect used for rendering
    GraphicsDevice GraphicsDevice; // Graphics device to draw with
    Texture2D heightMap; // Heightmap texture
}
```

The constructor will initialize many of these values:

```
public Terrain(Texture2D HeightMap, float CellSize, float Height,
    GraphicsDevice GraphicsDevice, ContentManager Content)
{
    this.heightMap = HeightMap;
    this.width = HeightMap.Width;
    this.length = HeightMap.Height;
```

```
        this.cellSize = CellSize;
        this.height = Height;

        this.GraphicsDevice = GraphicsDevice;

        effect = Content.Load<Effect>("TerrainEffect");

        // 1 vertex per pixel
        nVertices = width * length;

        // (Width-1) * (Length-1) cells, 2 triangles per cell, 3 indices per
        // triangle
        nIndices = (width - 1) * (length - 1) * 6;

        vertexBuffer = new VertexBuffer(GraphicsDevice,
            typeof(VertexPositionNormalTexture), nVertices,
                BufferUsage.WriteOnly);

          indexBuffer = new IndexBuffer(GraphicsDevice,
                            IndexElementSize.ThirtyTwoBits,
                            nIndices, BufferUsage.WriteOnly);
    }
```

Before we can generate any normals or indices, we need to know the dimensions of our grid. We know that the width and length are simply the width and height of our heightmap, but we need to extract the height values from the heightmap. We do this with the getHeights() function:

```
    private void getHeights()
    {
      // Extract pixel data
      Color[] heightMapData = new Color[width * length];
      heightMap.GetData<Color>(heightMapData);

      // Create heights[,] array
      heights = new float[width, length];

      // For each pixel
      for (int y = 0; y < length; y++)
        for (int x = 0; x < width; x++)
        {
          // Get color value (0 - 255)
          float amt = heightMapData[y * width + x].R;

          // Scale to (0 - 1)
```

```
        amt /= 255.0f;

        // Multiply by max height to get final height
        heights[x, y] = amt * height;
    }
}
```

This will initialize the `heights[,]` array, which we can then use to build our vertices. When building vertices, we simply lay out a vertex for each pixel in the heightmap, spaced according to the `cellSize` variable. Note that this will create *(width – 1) * (length – 1)* "cells" — each with two triangles:

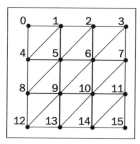

The function that does this is as shown:

```
private void createVertices()
{
  vertices = new VertexPositionNormalTexture[nVertices];

  // Calculate the position offset that will center the terrain at
  //    (0, 0, 0)
  Vector3 offsetToCenter = -new Vector3(((float)width / 2.0f) *
  cellSize, 0, ((float)length / 2.0f) * cellSize);

  // For each pixel in the image
  for (int z = 0; z < length; z++)
    for (int x = 0; x < width; x++)
    {
      // Find position based on grid coordinates and height in
      // heightmap
      Vector3 position = new Vector3(x * cellSize,
      heights[x, z], z * cellSize) + offsetToCenter;

      // UV coordinates range from (0, 0) at grid location (0, 0) to
      // (1, 1) at grid location (width, length)
      Vector2 uv = new Vector2((float)x / width, (float)z / length);
```

```
    // Create the vertex
    vertices[z * width + x] = new VertexPositionNormalTexture(
        position, Vector3.Zero, uv);
  }
}
```

When we create our terrain's index buffer, we need to lay out two triangles for each cell in the terrain. All we need to do is find the indices of the vertices at each corner of each cell, and create the triangles by specifying those indices in clockwise order for two triangles. For example, to create the triangles for the first cell in the preceding screenshot, we would specify the triangles as [0, 1, 4] and [4, 1, 5].

```
private void createIndices()
{
  indices = new int[nIndices];

  int i = 0;

  // For each cell
  for (int x = 0; x < width - 1; x++)
    for (int z = 0; z < length - 1; z++)
    {
      // Find the indices of the corners
      int upperLeft = z * width + x;
      int upperRight = upperLeft + 1;
      int lowerLeft = upperLeft + width;
      int lowerRight = lowerLeft + 1;

      // Specify upper triangle
      indices[i++] = upperLeft;
      indices[i++] = upperRight;
      indices[i++] = lowerLeft;

      // Specify lower triangle
      indices[i++] = lowerLeft;
      indices[i++] = upperRight;
      indices[i++] = lowerRight;
    }
}
```

The last thing we need to calculate for each vertex is the normals. Because we are creating the terrain from scratch, we will need to calculate all of the normals based only on the height data that we are given. This is actually much easier than it sounds: to calculate the normals we simply calculate the normal of each triangle of the terrain and add that normal to each vertex involved in the triangle. Once we have done this for each triangle, we simply normalize again, averaging the influences of each triangle connected to each vertex.

```
private void genNormals()
{
  // For each triangle
  for (int i = 0; i < nIndices; i += 3)
  {
    // Find the position of each corner of the triangle
    Vector3 v1 = vertices[indices[i]].Position;
    Vector3 v2 = vertices[indices[i + 1]].Position;
    Vector3 v3 = vertices[indices[i + 2]].Position;

    // Cross the vectors between the corners to get the normal
    Vector3 normal = Vector3.Cross(v1 - v2, v1 - v3);
    normal.Normalize();

    // Add the influence of the normal to each vertex in the
    // triangle
    vertices[indices[i]].Normal += normal;
    vertices[indices[i + 1]].Normal += normal;
    vertices[indices[i + 2]].Normal += normal;
  }

  // Average the influences of the triangles touching each
  // vertex
  for (int i = 0; i < nVertices; i++)
    vertices[i].Normal.Normalize();
}
```

We'll finish off the constructor by calling these functions in order and then setting the vertices and indices that we created into their respective buffers:

```
getHeights();
createVertices();
createIndices();
genNormals();

vertexBuffer.SetData<VertexPositionNormalTexture>(vertices);
indexBuffer.SetData<int>(indices);
```

Now that we've created the framework for this class, let's create the `TerrainEffect.fx` effect. This effect will, for the moment, be responsible for some simple directional lighting and texture mapping. We'll need a few `effect` parameters:

```
float4x4 View;
float4x4 Projection;

float3 LightDirection = float3(1, -1, 0);
float TextureTiling = 1;

texture2D BaseTexture;
sampler2D BaseTextureSampler = sampler_state {
    Texture = <BaseTexture>;
    AddressU = Wrap;
    AddressV = Wrap;
    MinFilter = Anisotropic;
    MagFilter = Anisotropic;
};
```

The `TextureTiling` parameter will determine how many times our texture is repeated across the terrain's surface—simply stretching it across the terrain would look bad because it would need to be stretched to a very large size. "Tiling" it across the terrain will look much better.

We will need a very standard vertex shader:

```
struct VertexShaderInput
{
  float4 Position : POSITION0;
  float2 UV : TEXCOORD0;
  float3 Normal : NORMAL0;
};

struct VertexShaderOutput
{
  float4 Position : POSITION0;
  float2 UV : TEXCOORD0;
  float3 Normal : TEXCOORD1;
};

VertexShaderOutput VertexShaderFunction(VertexShaderInput input)
{
  VertexShaderOutput output;

  output.Position = mul(input.Position, mul(View, Projection));
```

```
      output.Normal = input.Normal;
      output.UV = input.UV;

      return output;
}
```

The pixel shader is also very standard, except that we multiply the texture coordinates by the `TextureTiling` parameter. This works because the texture sampler's address mode is set to "wrap", and thus the sampler will simply wrap the texture coordinates past the edge of the texture, creating the tiling effect.

```
float4 PixelShaderFunction(VertexShaderOutput input) : COLOR0
{
    float light = dot(normalize(input.Normal),
                normalize(LightDirection));
    light = clamp(light + 0.4f, 0, 1); // Simple ambient lighting

    float3 tex = tex2D(BaseTextureSampler, input.UV * TextureTiling);

    return float4(tex * light, 1);
}
```

The technique definition is the same as our other effects:

```
technique Technique1
{
  pass Pass1
  {
     VertexShader = compile vs_2_0 VertexShaderFunction();
     PixelShader = compile ps_2_0 PixelShaderFunction();
  }
}
```

In order to use the effect with our terrain, we'll need to add a few more member variables to the `Terrain` class:

```
Texture2D baseTexture;
float textureTiling;
Vector3 lightDirection;
```

These values will be set from the constructor:

```
public Terrain(Texture2D HeightMap, float CellSize, float Height,
    Texture2D BaseTexture, float TextureTiling, Vector3 LightDirection,
    GraphicsDevice GraphicsDevice, ContentManager Content)
{
    this.baseTexture = BaseTexture;
```

```
this.textureTiling = TextureTiling;
this.lightDirection = LightDirection;

// etc...
```

Finally, we can simply set these `effect` parameters along with the `View` and `Projection` parameters in the `Draw()` function:

```
effect.Parameters["BaseTexture"].SetValue(baseTexture);
effect.Parameters["TextureTiling"].SetValue(textureTiling);
effect.Parameters["LightDirection"].SetValue(lightDirection);
```

Let's now add the terrain to our game. We'll need a new member variable in the `Game1` class:

```
Terrain terrain;
```

We'll need to initialize it in the `LoadContent()` method:

```
terrain = new Terrain(Content.Load<Texture2D>("terrain"), 30, 4800,
    Content.Load<Texture2D>("grass"), 6, new Vector3(1, -1, 0),
    GraphicsDevice, Content);
```

Finally, we can draw it in the `Draw()` function:

```
terrain.Draw(camera.View, camera.Projection);
```

Multitexturing

Our terrain looks pretty good as it is, but to make it more believable the texture applied to it needs to vary—snow and rocks at the peaks, for example. To do this, we will use a technique called **multitexturing**, which uses the red, blue, and green channels of a texture as a guide as to where to draw textures that correspond to those channels. For example, sand may correspond to red, snow to blue, and rock to green. Adding snow would then be as simple as painting blue onto the areas of this "texture map" that correspond with peaks on the heightmap. We will also have one extra texture that fills in the area where no colors have been painted onto the texture map—grass, for example.

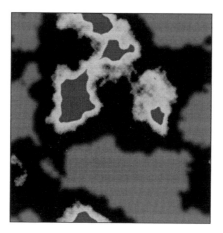

To begin with, we will need to modify our texture parameters on our effect from one texture to five: the texture map, the base texture, and the three color channel mapped textures.

```
texture RTexture;
sampler RTextureSampler = sampler_state
{
  texture = <RTexture>;
  AddressU = Wrap;
  AddressV = Wrap;
  MinFilter = Anisotropic;
  MagFilter = Anisotropic;
};

texture GTexture;
sampler GTextureSampler = sampler_state
{
  texture = <GTexture>;
```

```
  AddressU = Wrap;
  AddressV = Wrap;
  MinFilter = Anisotropic;
  MagFilter = Anisotropic;
};

texture BTexture;
sampler BTextureSampler = sampler_state
{
  texture = <BTexture>;
  AddressU = Wrap;
  AddressV = Wrap;
  MinFilter = Anisotropic;
  MagFilter = Anisotropic;
};

texture BaseTexture;
sampler BaseTextureSampler = sampler_state
{
  texture = <BaseTexture>;
  AddressU = Wrap;
  AddressV = Wrap;
  MinFilter = Anisotropic;
  MagFilter = Anisotropic;
};
texture WeightMap;
sampler WeightMapSampler = sampler_state {
  texture = <WeightMap>;
  AddressU = Clamp;
  AddressV = Clamp;
  MinFilter = Linear;
  MagFilter = Linear;
};
```

Second, we need to update our pixel shader to draw these textures onto the terrain:

```
float4 PixelShaderFunction(VertexShaderOutput input) : COLOR0
{
  float light = dot(normalize(input.Normal), normalize(
   LightDirection));
  light = clamp(light + 0.4f, 0, 1);

  float3 rTex = tex2D(RTextureSampler, input.UV * TextureTiling);
  float3 gTex = tex2D(GTextureSampler, input.UV * TextureTiling);
  float3 bTex = tex2D(BTextureSampler, input.UV * TextureTiling);
```

```
    float3 base = tex2D(BaseTextureSampler, input.UV * TextureTiling);

    float3 weightMap = tex2D(WeightMapSampler, input.UV);

    float3 output = clamp(1.0f - weightMap.r - weightMap.g -
      weightMap.b, 0, 1);
    output *= base;

    output += weightMap.r * rTex + weightMap.g * gTex +
      weightMap.b * bTex;

    return float4(output * light, 1);
}
```

We'll need to add a way to set these values to the Terrain class:

```
    public Texture2D RTexture, BTexture, GTexture, WeightMap;
```

All we need to do now is set these values to the effect in the Draw() function:

```
    effect.Parameters["RTexture"].SetValue(RTexture);
    effect.Parameters["GTexture"].SetValue(GTexture);
    effect.Parameters["BTexture"].SetValue(BTexture);
    effect.Parameters["WeightMap"].SetValue(WeightMap);
```

To use multitexturing in our game, we'll need to set these values in the Game1 class:

```
    terrain.WeightMap = Content.Load<Texture2D>("weightMap");
    terrain.RTexture = Content.Load<Texture2D>("sand");
    terrain.GTexture = Content.Load<Texture2D>("rock");
    terrain.BTexture = Content.Load<Texture2D>("snow");
```

Adding a detail texture to the terrain

Our last improvement to the terrain will be to add what is called a **detail texture**. This is essentially a noise texture that we blend in when the camera is close to the terrain to fake a higher resolution texture.

The terrain right now looks great from afar, but when the camera is close enough the texture will start to smudge and blur. However, if we increase the number of times the texture tiles, we start to see what is called **strobing**—where the high-resolution texture starts to flicker as it is scaled down in the distance. The easiest way to eliminate this effect is to just tile the main texture fewer times, but then we are left with a blurry texture up close as noted earlier. Adding a detail texture that fades in only when the camera is close to the terrain solves both of these problems. By multiplying the main texture(s) by the detail texture (which is tiled many more times across the terrain so that each tile is smaller and more detailed up close), we can make it look as though the main texture were higher resolution without getting the "strobe" effect at a distance.

To start with, we will need a few more `effect` parameters:

```
float DetailTextureTiling;
float DetailDistance = 2500;

texture DetailTexture;
sampler DetailSampler = sampler_state {
  texture = <DetailTexture>;
  AddressU = Wrap;
  AddressV = Wrap;
  MinFilter = Linear;
  MagFilter = Linear;
};
```

We can then update our pixel's shader to blend in the detail texture and multiply the output with it. The `lerp()` function interpolates between solid white (1) and the detail texture based on the depth at the pixel we're shading.

```
float3 detail = tex2D(DetailSampler, input.UV * DetailTextureTiling);
float detailAmt = input.Depth / DetailDistance;
detail = lerp(detail, 1, clamp(detailAmt, 0, 1));

return float4(detail * output * light, 1);
```

We'll need to add more instance variables to the `Terrain` class to reflect these parameters:

```
public Texture2D DetailTexture;
public float DetailDistance = 2500;
public float DetailTextureTiling = 100;
```

We also need to set these `effect` parameters in the `Draw()` function:

```
effect.Parameters["DetailTexture"].SetValue(DetailTexture);
effect.Parameters["DetailDistance"].SetValue(DetailDistance);
effect.Parameters["DetailTextureTiling"].SetValue(DetailTextureTiling
);
```

Finally, we'll set the `DetailTexture` value in the game's `LoadContent()` method:

```
terrain.DetailTexture = Content.Load<Texture2D>("noise_texture");
```

Placing plants on the terrain

The next step in building our environment is to add some plants and trees to the terrain. We will look at two approaches to placing billboards on the terrain, and we will use both approaches to add vegetation to the terrain—one for trees and one for grass. First, we will need a function to find the height of the terrain at any given coordinate. This is a deceptively complex problem as we will need to interpolate between the heights at each vertex rather than just retrieving a rounded value from the `heights` array. The function to do this is as follows. Note that it also outputs the "steepness" of the terrain at the sampled point—this value is simply the angle between the lower and higher of the vertices at the edge of the cell being sampled:

```
// Returns the height and steepness of the terrain at point (X, Z)
public float GetHeightAtPosition(float X, float Z, out float
Steepness)
{
  // Clamp coordinates to locations on terrain
  X = MathHelper.Clamp(X, (-width / 2) * cellSize,
     (width / 2) * cellSize);
  Z = MathHelper.Clamp(Z, (-length / 2) * cellSize,
     (length / 2) * cellSize);

  // Map from (-Width/2->Width/2,-Length/2->Length/2)
  // to (0->Width, 0->Length)
  X += (width / 2f) * cellSize;
  Z += (length / 2f) * cellSize;

  // Map to cell coordinates
  X /= cellSize;
  Z /= cellSize;

  // Truncate coordinates to get coordinates of top left cell vertex
  int x1 = (int)X;
  int z1 = (int)Z;

  // Try to get coordinates of bottom right cell vertex
  int x2 = x1 + 1 == width ? x1 : x1 + 1;
  int z2 = z1 + 1 == length ? z1 : z1 + 1;

  // Get the heights at the two corners of the cell
  float h1 = heights[x1, z1];
  float h2 = heights[x2, z2];

  // Determine steepness (angle between higher and lower vertex of
  // cell)
```

```
Steepness = (float)Math.Atan(Math.Abs((h1 - h2)) / (cellSize *
 Math.Sqrt(2)));

// Find the average of the amounts lost from coordinates during
// truncation above
float leftOver = ((X - x1) + (Z - z1)) / 2f;

// Interpolate between the corner vertices' heights
return MathHelper.Lerp(h1, h2, leftOver);
}
```

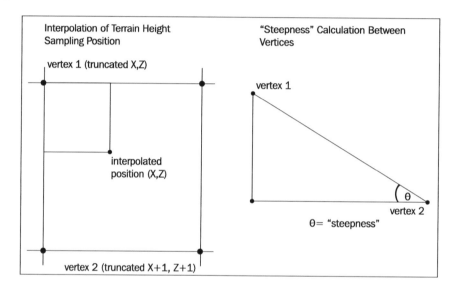

We can now use this function to place our trees randomly on the terrain. We will need a random number generator and a `BillboardSystem` in our `Game1` class:

```
Random r = new Random();
BillboardSystem trees;
```

When we get a random coordinate result from the random number generator, we will first check the height and steepness of the corresponding position on the terrain. If the steepness is more than 15 degrees or if the height does not fall into a reasonable range for trees to grow, we will reject the coordinates and try another random result. If we do find a good position for a tree, we simply add that position to the list to be drawn by the `BillboardSystem` we wrote in the last chapter. The following code, placed in the `LoadContent` function of the `Game1` class, will do this for us:

```
// Positions where trees should be drawn
List<Vector3> treePositions = new List<Vector3>();
```

```
// Continue until we get 500 trees on the terrain
for (int i = 0; i < 500; i++) // 500
{
  // Get X and Z coordinates from the random generator, between
  // [-(terrain width) / 2 * (cell size), (terrain width) / 2 * (cell
size)]
  float x = r.Next(-256 * 30, 256 * 30);
  float z = r.Next(-256 * 30, 256 * 30);

  // Get the height and steepness of this position on the terrain,
  // taking the height of the billboard into account
  float steepness;
  float y = terrain.GetHeightAtPosition(x, z, out steepness) + 100;

  // Reject this position if it is too low, high, or steep. Otherwise
  // add it to the list
  if (steepness < MathHelper.ToRadians(15) && y > 2300 && y < 3200)
    treePositions.Add(new Vector3(x, y, z));
  else
    i--;
}

trees = new BillboardSystem(GraphicsDevice, Content,
  Content.Load<Texture2D>("tree_billboard"), new Vector2(200),
  treePositions.ToArray());

trees.Mode = BillboardSystem.BillboardMode.Cylindrical;
trees.EnsureOcclusion = true;
```

Finally, we can draw the trees in the Draw() function:

```
trees.Draw(camera.View, camera.Projection, ((FreeCamera)camera).Up,
  ((FreeCamera)camera).Right);
```

We will now use a second method to add grass to the terrain. Here, we will use a texture as a "map" to dictate where to place the terrain. We could use the previous technique equally well, but the purpose here is more to demonstrate this technique. We will add a second billboard system to draw the grass billboards, and place them according to our map, where a brighter pixel means a higher chance of placing a grass billboard:

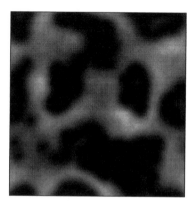

We'll need a second `BillboardSystem`:

```
BillboardSystem grass;
```

We initialize the `grass` value as follows:

```
// List of positions to place grass billboards
List<Vector3> grassPositions = new List<Vector3>();

// Retrieve pixel grid from grass map
Texture2D grassMap = Content.Load<Texture2D>("grass_map");
Color[] grassPixels = new Color[grassMap.Width * grassMap.Height];
grassMap.GetData<Color>(grassPixels);

// Loop until 1000 billboards have been placed
for (int i = 0; i < 300; i++)
{
  // Get X and Z coordinates from the random generator, between
  // [-(terrain width) / 2 * (cell size), (terrain width) / 2 * (cell
size)]
  float x = r.Next(-256 * 30, 256 * 30);
  float z = r.Next(-256 * 30, 256 * 30);

  // Get corresponding coordinates in grass map
```

```
int xCoord = (int)(x / 30) + 256;
int zCoord = (int)(z / 30) + 256;

// Get value between 0 and 1 from grass map
float texVal = grassPixels[zCoord * 512 + xCoord].R / 255f;

// Retrieve height
float steepness;
float y = terrain.GetHeightAtPosition(x, z, out steepness) + 50;

// Randomly place a billboard here based on pixel color in grass
// map
if ((int)((float)r.NextDouble() * texVal * 10) == 1)
  grassPositions.Add(new Vector3(x, y, z));
else
  i--;
}

// Create grass billboard system
grass = new BillboardSystem(GraphicsDevice, Content,
  Content.Load<Texture2D>("grass_billboard"), new Vector2(100),
  grassPositions.ToArray());

grass.Mode = BillboardSystem.BillboardMode.Cylindrical;
grass.EnsureOcclusion = false;
```

Again, we need to draw this billboard system in the Draw() function:

```
grass.Draw(camera.View, camera.Projection, ((FreeCamera)camera).Up,
  ((FreeCamera)camera).Right);
```

Adding the finishing touches

Our scene is starting to look pretty good! Let's finish it off by first adding a billboard system to render clouds, and finally bring in our sky and water effects. First, we will add a third billboard system for our clouds.

```
BillboardSystem clouds;
```

Note that the following function creates more believable clouds than in the last chapter by "clumping" billboards together instead of spreading them evenly across the sky.

```
List<Vector3> cloudPositions = new List<Vector3>();

// Create 20 "clusters" of clouds
for (int i = 0; i < 20; i++)
{
  Vector3 cloudLoc = new Vector3(r.Next(-8000, 8000),
    r.Next(4000, 6000), r.Next(-8000, 8000));

  // Add 10 cloud billboards around each cluster point
  for (int j = 0; j < 10; j++)
  {
    cloudPositions.Add(cloudLoc + new Vector3(r.Next(-3000, 3000),
      r.Next(-300, 900), r.Next(-1500, 1500)));
  }
}

clouds = new BillboardSystem(GraphicsDevice, Content,
  Content.Load<Texture2D>("cloud2"), new Vector2(2000),
cloudPositions.ToArray());

clouds.Mode = BillboardSystem.BillboardMode.Spherical;
clouds.EnsureOcclusion = false;
```

Once again, we'll need to draw the clouds in the `Draw()` function:

```
clouds.Draw(camera.View, camera.Projection, ((FreeCamera)camera).Up,
  ((FreeCamera)camera).Right);
```

Finally, let's add in water and a sky:

```
SkySphere sky;
Water water;
```

We'll initialize them as follows:

```
sky = new SkySphere(Content, GraphicsDevice,
 Content.Load<TextureCube>("clouds"));

water = new Water(Content, GraphicsDevice, new Vector3(0, 1600, 0),
   new Vector2(256 * 30));

water.Objects.Add(sky);
```

Now, we can update the Draw() function to draw everything:

```
// Called when the game should draw itself
protected override void Draw(GameTime gameTime)
{
  GraphicsDevice.Clear(Color.Black);
  water.PreDraw(camera, gameTime);

  GraphicsDevice.Clear(Color.Black);
  sky.Draw(camera.View, camera.Projection, ((FreeCamera)camera).
Position);

  foreach (CModel model in models)
     if (camera.BoundingVolumeIsInView(model.BoundingSphere))
        model.Draw(camera.View, camera.Projection,
        ((FreeCamera)camera).Position);

  terrain.Draw(camera.View, camera.Projection,
    ((FreeCamera)camera).Position);

  water.Draw(camera.View, camera.Projection,
    ((FreeCamera)camera).Position);

  trees.Draw(camera.View, camera.Projection, ((FreeCamera)camera).Up,
     ((FreeCamera)camera).Right);

  grass.Draw(camera.View, camera.Projection, ((FreeCamera)camera).Up,
     ((FreeCamera)camera).Right);

  clouds.Draw(camera.View, camera.Projection, ((FreeCamera)camera).Up,
     ((FreeCamera)camera).Right);

  base.Draw(gameTime);
}
```

There is one last thing we need to do—make the terrain `IRenderable`. We want the water to reflect the sky and the terrain, so we need to ensure that the `Water` class knows how to draw the terrain. We'll start by updating the `Terrain` class to include the `IRenderable` interface:

```
public class Terrain : IRenderable
```

We'll need to add a `SetClipPlane` function to this class as well:

```
public void SetClipPlane(Vector4? Plane)
{
    effect.Parameters["ClipPlaneEnabled"].SetValue(Plane.HasValue);

    if (Plane.HasValue)
        effect.Parameters["ClipPlane"].SetValue(Plane.Value);
}
```

Now, all we need to do is update the `TerrainEffect.fx` file to include clipping. First, we add the necessary `effect` parameters:

```
float4 ClipPlane;
bool ClipPlaneEnabled = false;
```

The `VertexShaderOutput` struct will now need to include the world space position:

```
float3 WorldPosition : TEXCOORD3;
```

We'll set this value in the vertex shader:

```
output.WorldPosition = input.Position;
```

Finally, we can perform the clipping at the beginning of the pixel shader:

```
if (ClipPlaneEnabled)
    clip(dot(float4(input.WorldPosition, 1), ClipPlane));
```

Finally, we can add the terrain to the list of items the water should reflect (in the `LoadContent()` function of the `Game1` class) and we're finished:

```
water.Objects.Add(terrain);
```

Summary

In this chapter, we learned a lot about environmental effects—terrain, clever placement of billboards, so-called "region growing" (placing billboards according to a texture)—and we also learned a lot about more advanced texturing techniques such as multitexturing and detail textures. We now have a very flexible terrain class, and a lovely environment to show it off in! In the next chapter, we will look at some post processing effects—blur, glow, and so on.

8
Advanced Materials and Post Processing

In this chapter, we will cover two topics: First, we will extend our `CModel` class to allow us to apply materials to objects per mesh rather than assigning materials to objects as a whole. This is important because often there are times where we do not want an entire model to have the same appearance. For example, the windows of a car shouldn't have the same reflectivity or transparency as the body of the car, or the tires or seats, but it would be a pain to try to work with each piece individually instead of as parts of a larger model, especially if we wanted to move the car, rotate it, and so on, and have each piece stay in position.

The second topic we will cover is post processing. A **post processing** effect is one applied to the rendered scene as a whole rather than one applied to individual objects in the scene. Basically, the full rendered scene as it would be drawn onto the screen is passed as an image to an `Effect` consisting only of a pixel shader. Instead of processing geometry, that `Effect` is processing only the pixels in an image. Post processing effects can be as simple as converting an image to black and white, or can be more complex, like a blur. In fact, the lighting calculation stage of our prelighting renderer is basically a post processor because it operates on the normals and depths of the scene stored in an image. We will create a framework for creating post processing effects, including a black and white effect, a full screen blur, a depth of field effect, and a glow effect.

Advanced Materials

XNA represents models as a set of meshes, which in turn are sets of "mesh parts." Each mesh part can have its own effect, texture, and so on. Because each mesh part can have a different effect, we will set up our CModel class to allow each mesh part to have its own effect and material. This will allow us to use different materials on different parts of the model: for example, rubber-like wheels and a shiny body on a car. Our MeshTag class already allows us to set the effect used on each mesh part, so we'll just extend this and also have it keep track of a material:

```
public Material Material = new Material();
```

Next, we'll add a function to the CModel class that will allow us to set a given effect to any given mesh part:

```
public void SetMeshEffect(string MeshName, Effect effect, bool
CopyEffect)
{
  foreach (ModelMesh mesh in Model.Meshes)
  {
    if (mesh.Name != MeshName)
      continue;

    foreach (ModelMeshPart part in mesh.MeshParts)
    {
      Effect toSet = effect;

      // Copy the effect if necessary
      if (CopyEffect)
        toSet = effect.Clone();

      MeshTag tag = ((MeshTag)part.Tag);

      // If this ModelMeshPart has a texture, set it to the effect
      if (tag.Texture != null)
      {
        setEffectParameter(toSet, "BasicTexture", tag.Texture);
        setEffectParameter(toSet, "TextureEnabled", true);
      }
      else
        setEffectParameter(toSet, "TextureEnabled", false);

      // Set our remaining parameters to the effect
      setEffectParameter(toSet, "DiffuseColor", tag.Color);
      setEffectParameter(toSet, "SpecularPower", tag.SpecularPower);

      part.Effect = toSet;
    }
  }
}
```

Similarly, we'll add a function to set a material to a given mesh part:

```
public void SetMeshMaterial(string MeshName, Material material)
{
  foreach (ModelMesh mesh in Model.Meshes)
  {
    if (mesh.Name != MeshName)
     continue;

    foreach (ModelMeshPart meshPart in mesh.MeshParts)
     ((MeshTag)meshPart.Tag).Material = material;
  }
}
```

We can also update the `SetModelEffect()` and `SetModelMaterial()` functions to use these functions:

```
public void SetModelEffect(Effect effect, bool CopyEffect)
{
  foreach (ModelMesh mesh in Model.Meshes)
    SetMeshEffect(mesh.Name, effect, CopyEffect);
}

public void SetModelMaterial(Material material)
{
  foreach (ModelMesh mesh in Model.Meshes)
    SetMeshMaterial(mesh.Name, material);
}
```

Finally, we can remove the effect-wide material and change the `draw` function to use the mesh part specific materials:

```
((MeshTag)meshPart.Tag).Material.SetEffectParameters(effect);
```

We could now use multiple materials on a model by setting our scene up as follows:

```
Effect lit = Content.Load<Effect>("LightingEffect");
Effect normal = Content.Load<Effect>("NormalMapEffect");

LightingMaterial marble = new LightingMaterial();
marble.SpecularColor = Color.White.ToVector3();

LightingMaterial steel = new LightingMaterial();
steel.SpecularColor = Color.Gray.ToVector3();

NormalMapMaterial brick = new NormalMapMaterial(
  Content.Load<Texture2D>("brick_normal_map"));

NormalMapMaterial wood = new NormalMapMaterial(
  Content.Load<Texture2D>("wood_normal"));
```

```
CModel model = new CModel(Content.Load<Model>("multimesh"),
    Vector3.Zero, Vector3.Zero, Vector3.One, GraphicsDevice);

model.SetMeshEffect("Box01", normal, true);
model.SetMeshMaterial("Box01", wood);

model.SetMeshEffect("Pyramid01", normal, true);
model.SetMeshMaterial("Pyramid01", brick);

model.SetMeshEffect("Sphere01", lit, true);
model.SetMeshMaterial("Sphere01", marble);

model.SetMeshEffect("Plane01", lit, true);
model.SetMeshMaterial("Plane01", steel);

models.Add(model);
```

Post processing

A post processor takes in an image and does some form of processing on it, whether it be desaturation of the image (converting to black and white), or averaging pixels and their neighbors to create a blur. Generally, the image that is processed is the rendered scene, so effects such as motion blur, glow, HDR bloom, and so on can be applied. However, it is also common to use post processors in intermediate stages of the rendering process—blurring a shadow map, for example.

Because we want to be able to implement many different kinds of post processing effects, we will create a framework that we can either use directly for simple post processing effects, or build on top of for more complex effects.

```
public class PostProcessor
{
}
```

Any post processing effect (as was mentioned at the beginning of the chapter) is basically a shader with only a pixel shader component. Thus, we will need an `Effect` instance to use that pixel shader. We also need a `Texture2D` to process:

```
// Pixel shader
public Effect Effect { get; protected set; }

// Texture to process
public Texture2D Input { get; set; }
```

We will also need a few other miscellaneous things—a `GraphicsDevice` and a `SpriteBatch`:

```
// GraphicsDevice and SpriteBatch for drawing
protected GraphicsDevice graphicsDevice;
protected static SpriteBatch spriteBatch;
```

The constructor will initialize these values:

```
public PostProcessor(Effect Effect, GraphicsDevice graphicsDevice)
{
  this.Effect = Effect;

  if (spriteBatch == null)
     spriteBatch = new SpriteBatch(graphicsDevice);

  this.graphicsDevice = graphicsDevice;
}
```

The `Draw()` function draws the texture with the effect applied:

```
// Draws the input texture using the pixel shader postprocessor
public virtual void Draw()
{
  // Set effect parameters if necessary
  if (Effect.Parameters["ScreenWidth"] != null)
     Effect.Parameters["ScreenWidth"].
       SetValue(graphicsDevice.Viewport.Width);

  if (Effect.Parameters["ScreenHeight"] != null)
     Effect.Parameters["ScreenHeight"].
       SetValue(graphicsDevice.Viewport.Height);

  // Initialize the spritebatch and effect
  spriteBatch.Begin(SpriteSortMode.Immediate, BlendState.Opaque);
  Effect.CurrentTechnique.Passes[0].Apply();
```

```
    // Draw the input texture
    spriteBatch.Draw(Input, Vector2.Zero, Color.White);

    // End the spritebatch and effect
    spriteBatch.End();

    // Clean up render states changed by the spritebatch
    graphicsDevice.DepthStencilState = DepthStencilState.Default;
    graphicsDevice.BlendState = BlendState.Opaque;
}
```

Next, we will create a class that will easily capture what is being drawn—in this case, to use as input to the post processor:

```
public class RenderCapture
{
  RenderTarget2D renderTarget;
  GraphicsDevice graphicsDevice;

  public RenderCapture(GraphicsDevice GraphicsDevice)
  {
    this.graphicsDevice = GraphicsDevice;
    renderTarget = new RenderTarget2D(GraphicsDevice,
    GraphicsDevice.Viewport.Width, GraphicsDevice.Viewport.Height,
      false, SurfaceFormat.Color, DepthFormat.Depth24);
  }

  // Begins capturing from the graphics device
  public void Begin()
  {
     graphicsDevice.SetRenderTarget(renderTarget);
  }

  // Stop capturing
  public void End()
  {
     graphicsDevice.SetRenderTarget(null);
  }

  // Returns what was captured
  public Texture2D GetTexture()
  {
    return renderTarget;
  }
}
```

We begin setting up the post processor by adding instance variables of the
`PostProcessor` and `RenderCapture` classes in the `Game1` class:

```
RenderCapture renderCapture;
PostProcessor postprocessor;
```

We initialize these two values in the `LoadContent()` function (we'll write the
`BWPostProcessor.fx` file in a moment):

```
renderCapture = new RenderCapture(GraphicsDevice);
postprocessor = new PostProcessor(Content.Load<Effect>
    ("BWPostProcessor"), GraphicsDevice);
```

Finally, we will use the `RenderCapture` to capture the initial render of the scene, and
use the `PostProcessor` to perform whatever effect it is performing:

```
// Called when the game should draw itself
protected override void Draw(GameTime gameTime)
{
  // Capture the render
  renderCapture.Begin();

  GraphicsDevice.Clear(Color.CornflowerBlue);

  // Draw all of the models
  foreach (CModel model in models)
    if (camera.BoundingVolumeIsInView(model.BoundingSphere))
        model.Draw(camera.View, camera.Projection,
        ((FreeCamera)camera).Position);

  // End capturing
  renderCapture.End();

  GraphicsDevice.Clear(Color.Black);

  // Perform postprocessing with the render of the scene
  postprocessor.Input = renderCapture.GetTexture();
  postprocessor.Draw();

  base.Draw(gameTime);
}
```

Black and white post processor

For our first post processing effect, we'll create a simple post processor that will convert the following screenshot (or any image) to grayscale (black and white).

We start by creating a new `Effect` file, with only a pixel shader:

```
float4 PixelShaderFunction(float4 Position : POSITION0,
  float2 UV : TEXCOORD0) : COLOR0
{
}

technique Technique1
{
  pass Pass1
  {
      PixelShader = compile ps_1_1 PixelShaderFunction();
  }
}
```

We need a way to access the input texture(s). To make this easy on ourselves, we will use an array of texture samplers instead of specifying each explicitly. We will see later how we set values to this array. For this shader, the `SpriteBatch` will set it for us automatically.

```
sampler2D tex[1]; // Input textures (just 1 in this case)
```

All we need to do now is add up the weighted values of each color channel. We weigh them because our eyes naturally pick up more information from the green channel, followed by red and blue roughly proportioned according to the weight values that we will use. This will allow us to get the clearest image possible because more useful information is stored in the green and red channels. We then set each pixel to the summed value to get a monotone image (black and white):

```
float4 PixelShaderFunction(float4 Position : POSITION0,
    float2 UV : TEXCOORD0) : COLOR0
{
  float4 color = tex2D(tex[0], UV);

  float intensity = 0.3f * color.r
      + 0.59f * color.g
      + 0.11f * color.b;

  return float4(intensity, intensity, intensity, color.a);
}
```

Our game is already set up to load and use this post processing effect, so we can simply run the game to see it at work:

Gaussian blur post processor

The next post processing effect that we will look at is blurring, specifically with what is called a "Gaussian" blur. A **Gaussian blur** is a blur which, instead of simply calculating a weighted average of a pixel and its neighbors, calculates a weighted average, weighing pixels based on their distance from the center pixel. The weights are calculated according to the Gaussian (or "normal") function:

$$G(x) = \frac{1}{\sqrt{2\pi\sigma}} e^{\frac{-x^2}{2\sigma^2}}$$

In normal use of this function, x is the distance from the mean of a data set, and σ is the standard deviation. In this case, x is a pixel's distance from the center pixel and σ is used as a parameter to determine how much the image is blurred. The following graph shows how much a pixel will be weighted as its distance approaches 1, 2, 3, and so on $\sigma's$ from the center pixel:

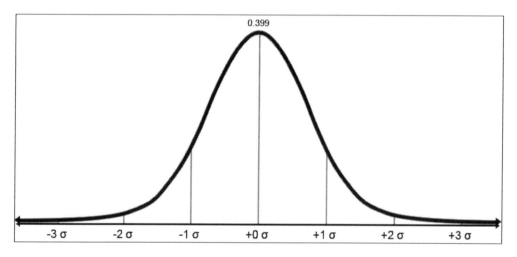

The `GaussianBlur` post processor is an extension of the basic `PostProcessor` class:

```
public class GaussianBlur : PostProcessor
{
}
```

We will sample from the input texture 15 times and calculate a weighted average of the sampled values. Thus, in addition to the overall blur amount parameter, we will store weights and offsets for each sample:

```
float blurAmount;

float[] weightsH, weightsV;
Vector2[] offsetsH, offsetsV;
```

We calculate the weights and offsets for the horizontal and vertical directions separately. Because a Gaussian blur can work in each direction independently, we perform the full blur in two passes—one blur horizontally and one blur vertically, giving us a stronger blur. The following function will calculate the weights and offsets for one pass:

```
void calcSettings(float w, float h, out float[] weights, out Vector2[]
offsets)
{
  // 15 Samples
  weights = new float[15];
  offsets = new Vector2[15];

  // Calculate values for center pixel
  weights[0] = gaussianFn(0);
  offsets[0] = new Vector2(0, 0);

  float total = weights[0];

  // Calculate samples in pairs
  for (int i = 0; i < 7; i++)
  {
      // Weight each pair of samples according to Gaussian function
      float weight = gaussianFn(i + 1);
      weights[i * 2 + 1] = weight;
      weights[i * 2 + 2] = weight;
      total += weight * 2;

      // Samples are offset by 1.5 pixels, to make use of
      // filtering halfway between pixels
      float offset = i * 2 + 1.5f;
      Vector2 offsetVec = new Vector2(w, h) * offset;
      offsets[i * 2 + 1] = offsetVec;
      offsets[i * 2 + 2] = -offsetVec;
  }

  // Divide all weights by total so they will add up to 1
  for (int i = 0; i < weights.Length; i++)
      weights[i] /= total;
}
```

This function makes use of the `gaussianFn()` function, which is an implementation of the previous mathematical function:

```
float gaussianFn(float x)
{
   return (float)((1.0f / Math.Sqrt(2 * Math.PI * blurAmount *
blurAmount)) *
      Math.Exp(-(x * x) / (2 * blurAmount * blurAmount)));
}
```

The `GaussianBlur` class will need a `RenderCapture` of its own to capture the output of the first blur pass, which it will then use as input to the second pass:

```
RenderCapture capture;
```

This value, along with the weights and offsets for each pass, will be initialized in the constructor:

```
public GaussianBlur(GraphicsDevice graphicsDevice,
   ContentManager Content,
   float BlurAmount) : base(Content.Load<Effect>
     ("GaussianBlur"), graphicsDevice)
{
   this.blurAmount = BlurAmount;

   // Calculate weights/offsets for horizontal pass
   calcSettings(1.0f / (float)graphicsDevice.Viewport.Width, 0,
      out weightsH, out offsetsH);

   // Calculate weights/offsets for vertical pass
   calcSettings(0, 1.0f / (float)graphicsDevice.Viewport.Height,
      out weightsV, out offsetsV);

   capture = new RenderCapture(graphicsDevice);
}
```

Finally, we perform the two blur passes in the overridden `Draw()` function:

```
public override void Draw()
{
   // Set values for horizontal pass
   Effect.Parameters["Offsets"].SetValue(offsetsH);
   Effect.Parameters["Weights"].SetValue(weightsH);

   // Render this pass into the RenderCapture
```

```
capture.Begin();
base.Draw();
capture.End();

// Get the results of the first pass
Input = capture.GetTexture();

// Set values for the vertical pass
Effect.Parameters["Offsets"].SetValue(offsetsV);
Effect.Parameters["Weights"].SetValue(weightsV);

// Render the final pass
base.Draw();
}
```

The next step is to write the Gaussian blur effect file. Again, we'll need a texture sampler array. Additionally, we will need `effect` parameters for our weight and offset values:

```
sampler2D tex[1];

float2 Offsets[15];
float Weights[15];
```

The pixel shader performs 15 texture lookups based on the offsets from the main pixel being shaded, and weighs the results based on the weights calculated by the `Gaussian` function:

```
float4 PixelShaderFunction(float4 Position : POSITION0,
    float2 UV : TEXCOORD0) : COLOR0
{
   float4 output = float4(0, 0, 0, 1);

   for (int i = 0; i < 15; i++)
       output += tex2D(tex[0], UV + Offsets[i]) * Weights[i];

   return output;
}
```

The technique definition simply defines the pixel shader:

```
technique Technique1
{
   pass p0
   {
       PixelShader = compile ps_2_0 PixelShaderFunction();
   }
}
```

All we need to do to use this in our game is change our black and white PostProcessor class to a GaussianBlur:

```
postprocessor = new GaussianBlur(GraphicsDevice, Content, 2);
```

Depth of field

The next effect that we will look at builds on our Gaussian blur effect to recreate the "depth of field" effect. In the real world, cameras have one specific range they can focus clearly on, and everything outside of that range is blurred somewhat, getting increasingly blurry as the subjects move farther from the focal range. Generally, the effect isn't terribly noticeable, but in some cases it can be exaggerated intentionally for aesthetic effects.

The process is simple: First, we render the scene storing only the depth values in a depth map (like we did in *Chapter 3, Advanced Lighting*). Then we render the scene normally, storing both the original render and a blurred version of it. Finally, we combine the blurred and non-blurred images in another post processor, which determines how much to blur the image based on the depths stored in the depth map at each pixel.

The effect that we will need to render the depth map is very simple, and we have seen most if not all of it before:

```
float4x4 World;
float4x4 View;
float4x4 Projection;
```

```
float MaxDepth = 20000;

struct VertexShaderInput
{
   float4 Position : POSITION0;
};

struct VertexShaderOutput
{
   float4 Position : POSITION0;
   float Depth : TEXCOORD0;
};

VertexShaderOutput VertexShaderFunction(VertexShaderInput input)
{
  VertexShaderOutput output;

   // Output position and depth
   output.Position = mul(input.Position, mul(World, mul(View,
Projection)));
   output.Depth = output.Position.z;

   return output;
}

float4 PixelShaderFunction(VertexShaderOutput input) : COLOR0
{
   // Return depth, scaled/clamped to [0, 1]
   return float4(input.Depth / MaxDepth, 0, 0, 1);
}

technique Technique1
{
  pass Pass1
  {
     VertexShader = compile vs_2_0 VertexShaderFunction();
     PixelShader = compile ps_2_0 PixelShaderFunction();
  }
}
```

For simplicity's sake, we will render the depth map directly in the Game1 class. We will need to load the effect that we have just created and a RenderCapture:

```
RenderCapture depthCapture;
Effect depthEffect;
```

These values will be initialized in the LoadContent() function:

```
depthEffect = Content.Load<Effect>("DepthEffect");
depthCapture = new RenderCapture(GraphicsDevice, SurfaceFormat.
HalfSingle);
```

We will then use these to start off the Draw() function by rendering the depth map:

```
// Start rendering to depth map
depthCapture.Begin();

// Clear to white (max depth)
GraphicsDevice.Clear(Color.White);

foreach(CModel model in models)
  if (camera.BoundingVolumeIsInView(model.BoundingSphere))
  {
    model.CacheEffects(); // Cache effect
    model.SetModelEffect(depthEffect, false); // Set depth effect
    model.Draw(camera.View, camera.Projection,
      ((FreeCamera)camera).Position);
    model.RestoreEffects(); // Restore effects
  }
```

```
// Finish rendering to depth map
depthCapture.End();
```

In the next step, we will render the scene as usual, into our existing
RenderCapture:
```
// Begin rendering the main render
renderCapture.Begin();

GraphicsDevice.Clear(Color.CornflowerBlue);

// Draw all models
foreach (CModel model in models)
   if (camera.BoundingVolumeIsInView(model.BoundingSphere))
       model.Draw(camera.View, camera.Projection, ((FreeCamera)camera).
Position);

// Finish the main render
renderCapture.End();
```

The next step is to blur the rendered scene. However, our GaussianBlur class will
output only its results directly to the screen. We could try wrapping its draw call
with a RenderCapture, but this will not work as it uses a RenderCapture of its own
internally to capture the results of its first pass. What we need to do is capture the
results of its second pass, so we will have to have the GaussianBlur class do this for
us. Let's add a value to the GaussianBlur class that will allow us to specify where
we want to send its output:

```
public RenderCapture ResultCapture = null;
```

If this value is set to null when the Draw() function of GaussianBlur is called, it will
simply output the results of its second pass directly to the screen. Otherwise, it will
render into whichever RenderCapture is specified:

```
if (ResultCapture != null)
  ResultCapture.Begin();

// Set values for the vertical pass
Effect.Parameters["Offsets"].SetValue(offsetsV);
Effect.Parameters["Weights"].SetValue(weightsV);

// Render the final pass
base.Draw();

if (ResultCapture != null)
  ResultCapture.End();
```

To capture the results of the blur, the `Game1` class will need another `RenderCapture`:

```
RenderCapture blurCapture;
```

This `RenderCapture` will need to be initialized in the `LoadContent()` function:

```
blurCapture = new RenderCapture(GraphicsDevice, SurfaceFormat.Color);
```

Now, we can continue the `Draw()` function by blurring the main render:

```
// Prepare to blur results of main render
postprocessor.Input = renderCapture.GetTexture();
// Output blur to our RenderCapture
((GaussianBlur)postprocessor).ResultCapture = blurCapture;
// Perform blur
postprocessor.Draw();
```

Now that we've rendered all of these various views of the scene, we need to combine them into the final result. We will do this with another `PostProcessor` called `DepthOfField`, whose main role is to handle setting all three textures to the `GraphicsDevice` and loading the `Effect` that combines them:

```
public class DepthOfField : PostProcessor
{
  // Depth map and un-blurred render of scene. The blurred render
  // will be set as the Input value
  public Texture2D DepthMap;
  public Texture2D Unblurred;

  public DepthOfField(GraphicsDevice graphicsDevice,
    ContentManager Content): base(Content.Load<Effect>
      ("DepthOfField"), graphicsDevice)
  {
  }

  public override void Draw()
  {
    // Set the two textures above to the second and third
    // texture slots
    graphicsDevice.Textures[1] = Unblurred;
    graphicsDevice.Textures[2] = DepthMap;

    // Set the samplers for all three textures to PointClamp
    // so we can sample pixel values directly
    graphicsDevice.SamplerStates[0] = SamplerState.PointClamp;
    graphicsDevice.SamplerStates[1] = SamplerState.PointClamp;
    graphicsDevice.SamplerStates[2] = SamplerState.PointClamp;

    base.Draw();
  }
}
```

Finally, the `effect` file simply samples the depth from the depth map and converts it back to its full range. It then samples the blurred and non-blurred copies of the scene, and blends between them using essentially the same calculations that we used to draw fog in the earlier chapters:

```
sampler2D tex[3];

float MaxDepth = 20000;

// Distance at which blur starts
float BlurStart = 600;

// Distance at which scene is fully blurred
float BlurEnd = 1000;

float4 PixelShaderFunction(float4 Position : POSITION0,
    float2 UV : TEXCOORD0) : COLOR0
{
    // Determine depth
    float depth = tex2D(tex[2], UV).r * MaxDepth;

    // Get blurred and unblurred render of scene
    float4 unblurred = tex2D(tex[1], UV);
    float4 blurred = tex2D(tex[0], UV);

    // Determine blur amount (similar to fog calculation)
    float blurAmt = clamp((depth - BlurStart) / (BlurEnd - BlurStart),
       0, 1);

    // Blend between unblurred and blurred images
    float4 mix = lerp(unblurred, blurred, blurAmt);

    return mix;
}

technique Technique1
{
  pass p0
  {
      PixelShader = compile ps_2_0 PixelShaderFunction();
  }
}
```

All we need to do now is create an instance of this class in the `Game1` class:

```
DepthOfField dof;
```

We will set it up in the `LoadContent()` function:

```
dof = new DepthOfField(GraphicsDevice, Content);
```

Finally, we can finish off the `Draw()` function by using the `DepthOfField` class to combine all of the images into the final result. We must also be sure to call `base.Draw()` when we are done:

```
// Set the three images to the DOF class
dof.DepthMap = depthCapture.GetTexture();
dof.Unblurred = renderCapture.GetTexture();
dof.Input = ((GaussianBlur)postprocessor).ResultCapture.GetTexture();

// Combine the images into the final result
dof.Draw();

base.Draw(gameTime);
```

This finishes up the depth of the field effect. Notice when running the game that objects that are close to the camera stay entirely in focus, and fade to a blur between the `FogStart` and `FogEnd` ranges. In a "real" implementation of the depth of field, these values would change while the camera was moved to focus on different objects. For example, depth of field is often used in game cinematics, focusing on a character who is talking and blurring the scene behind them. Depth of field can also be useful for a weapon scope effect, focusing on the object the player is currently targeting, for example. In that case, we would simply cast a ray into the scene to determine the depth at which we want to start the blur.

Glow post processor

The final effect that we will look at is **glow**. Glow is generally implemented by
rendering the parts of the scene that are meant to glow into a render target, then
blurring that render target. The blurred image is then drawn additively over the
original render of the scene to make it look like parts of the scene are in fact emitting
light. The following screenshot shows the non-blurred glow channel on the left,
which transitions to the blurred version on the right:

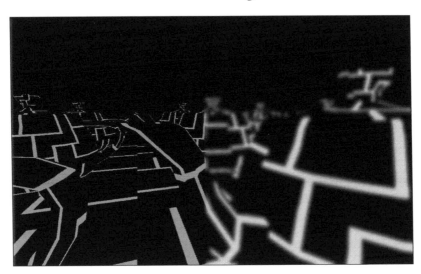

We will need a few things to implement glow in our game: RenderCapture for the
regular render of the scene and the glow render, an effect to used to render the glow,
and a GaussianBlur to blur the glowing scene.

```
RenderCapture renderCapture;
RenderCapture glowCapture;
Effect glowEffect;
GaussianBlur blur;
```

We set these values up as follows in the LoadContent() function:
```
renderCapture = new RenderCapture(GraphicsDevice);
glowCapture = new RenderCapture(GraphicsDevice);

glowEffect = Content.Load<Effect>("GlowEffect");
glowEffect.Parameters["GlowTexture"].SetValue(
    Content.Load<Texture2D>("glow_map"));

blur = new GaussianBlur(GraphicsDevice, Content, 4);
```

The contents of the `GlowEffect.fx` effect are very simple, no more complicated than drawing a texture onto a model—the same way we did back in *Chapter 2, Introduction to HLSL*:

```
float4x4 World;
float4x4 View;
float4x4 Projection;

texture GlowTexture;

sampler2D GlowSampler = sampler_state {
    texture = <GlowTexture>;
};

struct VertexShaderInput
{
    float4 Position : POSITION0;
    float2 UV : TEXCOORD0;
};

struct VertexShaderOutput
{
    float4 Position : POSITION0;
    float2 UV : TEXCOORD0;
};

VertexShaderOutput VertexShaderFunction(VertexShaderInput input)
{
    VertexShaderOutput output;

    output.Position = mul(input.Position, mul(World,
        mul(View, Projection)));
    output.UV = input.UV;

    return output;
}

float4 PixelShaderFunction(VertexShaderOutput input) : COLOR0
{
    return tex2D(GlowSampler, input.UV);
}

technique Technique1
{
```

```
    pass Pass1
    {
        VertexShader = compile vs_2_0 VertexShaderFunction();
        PixelShader = compile ps_2_0 PixelShaderFunction();
    }
}
```

Now all we need to do is update the `Draw()` function. We begin drawing by rendering the glowing scene to the corresponding `RenderCapture`:

```
// Begin capturing the glow render
glowCapture.Begin();

GraphicsDevice.Clear(Color.Black);

// Draw all models with the glow effect/texture applied, reverting
// the effect when finished
foreach (CModel model in models)
  if (camera.BoundingVolumeIsInView(model.BoundingSphere))
  {
    model.CacheEffects();
    model.SetModelEffect(glowEffect, false);
    model.Draw(camera.View, camera.Projection,
      ((FreeCamera)camera).Position);
    model.RestoreEffects();
  }

// Finish capturing the glow
glowCapture.End();
```

Next, we draw the scene as usual into the second `RenderCapture`:

```
// Draw the scene regularly into the other RenderCapture
renderCapture.Begin();

GraphicsDevice.Clear(Color.Black);

// Draw all models
foreach (CModel model in models)
  if (camera.BoundingVolumeIsInView(model.BoundingSphere))
      model.Draw(camera.View, camera.Projection,
        ((FreeCamera)camera).Position);

// Finish capturing
renderCapture.End();
```

Next, we blur the glow render, storing the result into the same RenderCapture:

```
// Blur the glow render back into the glow RenderCapture
blur.Input = glowCapture.GetTexture();
blur.ResultCapture = glowCapture;
blur.Draw();
```

Finally, we simply draw the two renderers of the scene on top of each other with the SpriteBatch, making sure to blend additively so that the glowing areas of the scene will brighten the image:

```
// Draw the blurred glow render over the normal render additively
spriteBatch.Begin(SpriteSortMode.Immediate, BlendState.Additive);
spriteBatch.Draw(renderCapture.GetTexture(), Vector2.Zero, Color.White);
spriteBatch.Draw(glowCapture.GetTexture(), Vector2.Zero, Color.White);
spriteBatch.End();

// Clean up after the SpriteBatch
GraphicsDevice.DepthStencilState = DepthStencilState.Default;
GraphicsDevice.BlendState = BlendState.Opaque;

base.Draw(gameTime);
```

Summary

Having finished this chapter, we have extended the CModel class to allow us to set materials and effects to individual meshes rather than limiting us to setting these only to models as a whole. We have also created a flexible framework for implementing various post processing effects, and have implemented a number of post processing effects of our own, including a black and white filter, a full screen blur, depth of field, and glow.

In the next and the final chapter of the book we will look at various topics in animation, including animation of objects as a whole (moving a vehicle around a track, for example), animation of specific meshes of a model (spinning the blades on a windmill, for example), and what is called "skinned animation"—animation of the bones in a model that causes the model itself to deform. This is useful for character animation, where the "skin" of the model will bend, stretch, and flex along with the model's bones.

9
Animation

In this chapter, we will look at several ways to make the objects in our scene move. First, we will look at the animation of objects as a whole. We will do this through simple linear interpolation between start and end values, and through a more complex curve interpolation. We will also look at more complex animations through **keyframed animation**. We will look at **hierarchical** animation to animate specific pieces of a model, and finally, we will look at **skinned animation**—the animation of the vertices of a model themselves according to the model's skeletal structure.

Object animation

We will first look at the animation of objects as a whole. The most common ways to animate an object are rotation and translation (movement). We will begin by creating a class that will interpolate a position and rotation value between two extremes over a given amount of time. We could also have it interpolate between two scaling values, but it is very uncommon for an object to change size in a smooth manner during gameplay, so we will leave it out for simplicity's sake.

The `ObjectAnimation` class has a number of parameters—starting and ending position and rotation values, a duration to interpolate during those values, and a Boolean indicating whether or not the animation should loop or just remain at the end value after the duration has passed:

```
public class ObjectAnimation
{
  Vector3 startPosition, endPosition, startRotation, endRotation;
  TimeSpan duration;
  bool loop;
}
```

We will also store the amount of time that has elapsed since the animation began, and the current position and rotation values:

```
TimeSpan elapsedTime = TimeSpan.FromSeconds(0);


public Vector3 Position { get; private set; }
public Vector3 Rotation { get; private set; }
```

The constructor will initialize these values:

```
public ObjectAnimation(Vector3 StartPosition, Vector3 EndPosition,
    Vector3 StartRotation, Vector3 EndRotation, TimeSpan Duration,
    bool Loop)
{
    this.startPosition = StartPosition;
    this.endPosition = EndPosition;
    this.startRotation = StartRotation;
    this.endRotation = EndRotation;
    this.duration = Duration;
    this.loop = Loop;
    Position = startPosition;
    Rotation = startRotation;
}
```

Finally, the `Update()` function takes the amount of time that has elapsed since the last update and updates the position and rotation values accordingly:

```
public void Update(TimeSpan Elapsed)
{
    // Update the time
    this.elapsedTime += Elapsed;

    // Determine how far along the duration value we are (0 to 1)
    float amt = (float)elapsedTime.TotalSeconds / (float)duration.
TotalSeconds;

    if (loop)
        while (amt > 1) // Wrap the time if we are looping
            amt -= 1;
    else // Clamp to the end value if we are not
        amt = MathHelper.Clamp(amt, 0, 1);

    // Update the current position and rotation
    Position = Vector3.Lerp(startPosition, endPosition, amt);
    Rotation = Vector3.Lerp(startRotation, endRotation, amt);
}
```

As a simple example, we'll create an animation (in the `Game1` class) that rotates our spaceship in a circle over a few seconds:

Object Animation

We'll also have it move the model up and down for demonstration's sake:

```
ObjectAnimation anim;
```

We initialize it in the constructor:

```
models.Add(new CModel(Content.Load<Model>("ship"),
    Vector3.Zero, Vector3.Zero, new Vector3(0.25f), GraphicsDevice));

anim = new ObjectAnimation(new Vector3(0, -150, 0),
    new Vector3(0, 150, 0),
    Vector3.Zero, new Vector3(0, -MathHelper.TwoPi, 0),
    TimeSpan.FromSeconds(10), true);
```

We update it as follows:

```
anim.Update(gameTime.ElapsedGameTime);

models[0].Position = anim.Position;
models[0].Rotation = anim.Rotation;
```

Keyframed animation

Our `ObjectAnimation` class allows us to create simple linear animations, but we can't create anything more complex. For example, we can't make our spaceship move in a circle with this class. To achieve more complex animations, we will use what is called **keyframed animation**. In this method, we specify "key" frames where we want the object to be in a specific position and orientation. We then rely on the code to interpolate between those values to fill in the frames between the key frames.

The following screenshot shows our spaceship at the keyframed positions along a path, and the black line shows the path that would be taken by interpolating between keyframes:

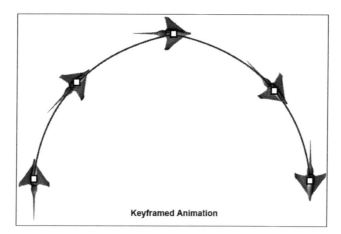

Keyframed Animation

Keyframed animation is useful because it is a fast way to create somewhat complex animations without having to animate each frame. For example, birds flying through the air, soldiers on patrol, or even a camera flying through a scene, can all be animated through keyframes. This is probably the easiest way to move the camera during a cutscene, for example. We represent a key frame with the `ObjectAnimationFrame` class. Like the previous class, it contains position and rotation values. It also, however, contains a time value, marking this frame's time offset from the beginning of the animation.

```
public class ObjectAnimationFrame
{
    public Vector3 Position { get; private set; }
    public Vector3 Rotation { get; private set; }
    public TimeSpan Time { get; private set; }

    public ObjectAnimationFrame(Vector3 Position, Vector3 Rotation,
      TimeSpan Time)
    {
        this.Position = Position;
        this.Rotation = Rotation;
        this.Time = Time;
    }
}
```

We can now create a new animation class that uses key frames:

```
public class KeyframedObjectAnimation
{
  List<ObjectAnimationFrame> frames = new List<ObjectAnimationFrame>();
  bool loop;
  TimeSpan elapsedTime = TimeSpan.FromSeconds(0);

  public Vector3 Position { get; private set; }
  public Vector3 Rotation { get; private set; }

  public KeyframedObjectAnimation(List<ObjectAnimationFrame> Frames,
   bool Loop)
  {
    this.frames = Frames;
     this.loop = Loop;
    Position = Frames[0].Position;
    Rotation = Frames[0].Rotation;
  }
}
```

Finally, the Update() function figures out which frame we are on and interpolates between its values and the next frame's values, based on how far between them we are:

```
public void Update(TimeSpan Elapsed)
{
  // Update the time
  this.elapsedTime += Elapsed;

  TimeSpan totalTime = elapsedTime;
  TimeSpan end = frames[frames.Count - 1].Time;

  if (loop) // Loop around the total time if necessary
    while (totalTime > end)
        totalTime -= end;
  else // Otherwise, clamp to the end values
  {
    Position = frames[frames.Count - 1].Position;
    Rotation = frames[frames.Count - 1].Rotation;
    return;
  }

  int i = 0;
```

```
    // Find the index of the current frame
    while(frames[i + 1].Time < totalTime)
        i++;

    // Find the time since the beginning of this frame
    totalTime -= frames[i].Time;

    // Find how far we are between the current and next frame (0 to 1)
    float amt = (float)((totalTime.TotalSeconds) /
        (frames[i + 1].Time - frames[i].Time).TotalSeconds);

    // Interpolate position and rotation values between frames
    Position = Vector3.Lerp(frames[i].Position, frames[i + 1].Position,
        amt);
    Rotation = Vector3.Lerp(frames[i].Rotation, frames[i + 1].Rotation,
        amt);
}
```

For example, we can now create a new animation to move our spaceship in a square:

```
KeyframedObjectAnimation anim;
```

We set it up as follows:

```
List<ObjectAnimationFrame> frames = new List<ObjectAnimationFrame>();

frames.Add(new ObjectAnimationFrame(new Vector3(-1000, 100, -1000),
    new Vector3(0, MathHelper.ToRadians(-90), 0),
    TimeSpan.FromSeconds(0)));
frames.Add(new ObjectAnimationFrame(new Vector3(1000, 100, -1000),
    new Vector3(0, MathHelper.ToRadians(-90), 0),
    TimeSpan.FromSeconds(3)));
frames.Add(new ObjectAnimationFrame(new Vector3(1000, 100, -1000),
    new Vector3(0, MathHelper.ToRadians(-180), 0),
    TimeSpan.FromSeconds(6)));
frames.Add(new ObjectAnimationFrame(new Vector3(1000, 100, 1000),
    new Vector3(0, MathHelper.ToRadians(-180), 0),
    TimeSpan.FromSeconds(9)));
frames.Add(new ObjectAnimationFrame(new Vector3(1000, 100, 1000),
    new Vector3(0, MathHelper.ToRadians(-270), 0),
    TimeSpan.FromSeconds(12)));
frames.Add(new ObjectAnimationFrame(new Vector3(-1000, 100, 1000),
    new Vector3(0, MathHelper.ToRadians(-270), 0),
    TimeSpan.FromSeconds(15)));
frames.Add(new ObjectAnimationFrame(new Vector3(-1000, 100, 1000),
    new Vector3(0, MathHelper.ToRadians(-360), 0),
    TimeSpan.FromSeconds(18)));
```

```
frames.Add(new ObjectAnimationFrame(new Vector3(-1000, 100, -1000),
    new Vector3(0, MathHelper.ToRadians(-360), 0),
    TimeSpan.FromSeconds(21)));
frames.Add(new ObjectAnimationFrame(new Vector3(-1000, 100, -1000),
    new Vector3(0, MathHelper.ToRadians(-450), 0),
    TimeSpan.FromSeconds(24)));

anim = new KeyframedObjectAnimation(frames, true);
```

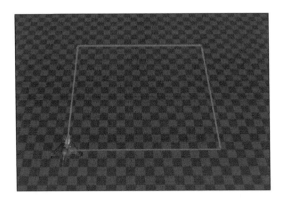

The Update code remains the same. Running the game, you will see the spaceship move from corner to corner of a box, turning towards the next corner at each stop.

Curve interpolation

We now have the ability to make animations with multiple key frames, which allows us to create more complex animations. However, we are still interpolating linearly between those key frames. This looks good for rotations, for example, but it would not look good for an object following a path, as the object would abruptly change direction after reaching a key frame in its animation. Instead, we want to be able to have our objects follow a smooth curve through the positions defined in the key frames. We will do this with what is called **Catmull-Rom interpolation**. This is a process that will create a curve through our key frame positions, allowing for much smoother object animation:

Let's modify the `KeyframedObjectAnimation` class to use Catmull-Rom interpolation for the position value. XNA has a built-in function to calculate an interpolated position between the second and third points in a set of four points using Catmull-rom interpolation. However, it works only in one dimension, so we'll need to create a function that will interpolate between a set of instances of `Vector3`:

```
Vector3 catmullRom3D(Vector3 v1, Vector3 v2, Vector3 v3, Vector3 v4,
float amt)
{
  return new Vector3(
    MathHelper.CatmullRom(v1.X, v2.X, v3.X, v4.X, amt),
    MathHelper.CatmullRom(v1.Y, v2.Y, v3.Y, v4.Y, amt),
    MathHelper.CatmullRom(v1.Z, v2.Z, v3.Z, v4.Z, amt));
}
```

The `amt` argument specifies how far (0 to 1) between the second and third vectors the new position should be. We can now modify the position calculation to use this new function:

```
// Interpolate position and rotation values between frames
Position = catmullRom3D(frames[wrap(i - 1, frames.Count - 1)].
Position,
  frames[wrap(i, frames.Count - 1)].Position,
  frames[wrap(i + 1, frames.Count - 1)].Position,
  frames[wrap(i + 2, frames.Count - 1)].Position, amt);
```

The `wrap()` function wraps the value that it is given around a certain interval—in this case [0, `frames.Count` - 1]. This means that we will not have to worry about our indices going out of range when finding the last point, next point, and so on, but it does mean that this type of interpolation will work best with a closed curve—a circle, for example:

```
// Wraps the "value" argument around [0, max]
int wrap(int value, int max)
{
  while (value > max)
    value -= max;

  while (value < 0)
    value += max;

  return value;
}
```

We could now create the following keyframed animation with a curved path to demonstrate our new interpolation method:

```
List<ObjectAnimationFrame> frames = new List<ObjectAnimationFrame>();

frames.Add(new ObjectAnimationFrame(new Vector3(-500, 100, 1000),
    new Vector3(0, MathHelper.ToRadians(0), 0),
    TimeSpan.FromSeconds(0)));
frames.Add(new ObjectAnimationFrame(new Vector3(500, 100, 500),
    new Vector3(0, MathHelper.ToRadians(0), 0),
    TimeSpan.FromSeconds(3)));
frames.Add(new ObjectAnimationFrame(new Vector3(-500, 100, 0),
    new Vector3(0, MathHelper.ToRadians(0), 0),
    TimeSpan.FromSeconds(6)));
frames.Add(new ObjectAnimationFrame(new Vector3(500, 100, -500),
    new Vector3(0, MathHelper.ToRadians(0), 0),
    TimeSpan.FromSeconds(9)));
frames.Add(new ObjectAnimationFrame(new Vector3(-500, 100, -1000),
    new Vector3(0, MathHelper.ToRadians(180), 0),
    TimeSpan.FromSeconds(12)));
frames.Add(new ObjectAnimationFrame(new Vector3(-500, 100, 1000),
    new Vector3(0, MathHelper.ToRadians(180), 0),
    TimeSpan.FromSeconds(15)));
frames.Add(new ObjectAnimationFrame(new Vector3(-500, 100, 1000),
    new Vector3(0, MathHelper.ToRadians(360), 0),
    TimeSpan.FromSeconds(18)));

anim = new KeyframedObjectAnimation(frames, true);
```

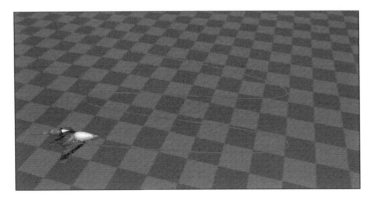

Building a Race Track from a Curve

Our method of Catmull-Rom curve interpolation works well for moving objects along a smooth path, but can also be used for many other things. In this example, we will build a race track from a curve and have a car follow that path at the player's command. The `RaceTrack` class will take care of creating and rendering the track:

```
public class RaceTrack
{
  // List of control points
  List<Vector2> positions;

  // Vertex and index buffers
  VertexBuffer vb;
  IndexBuffer ib;
  int nVertices, nIndices;

  // Rendering variables
  GraphicsDevice graphicsDevice;
  BasicEffect effect;
  Texture2D texture;

  // Total length of the track
  float trackLength;
}
```

Note that we store the positions as a list of instances of `Vector2`, as the track is flat on the ground and requires no Y position component. The constructor will direct the initialization of the track:

```
public RaceTrack(List<Vector2> positions, int nDivisions, float
trackWidth, int textureRepetitions, GraphicsDevice graphicsDevice,
  ContentManager content)
{
  this.graphicsDevice = graphicsDevice;
  this.positions = interpolatePositions(positions, nDivisions);

  effect = new BasicEffect(graphicsDevice);
  texture = content.Load<Texture2D>("track");

  createBuffers(trackWidth, textureRepetitions);
}
```

The constructor first calls the `interpolatePositions()` function, which adds a given number of points to the list of control points based on Catmull-Rom interpolation. We've already seen most of this in the last section—we are simply using a similar `Catmull-Rom` function to insert extra positions into a list:

```
// Adds the given number of positions between the control points
specified,
// to subdivide/smooth the path
List<Vector2> interpolatePositions(List<Vector2> positions, int
nDivisions)
{
  // Create a new list of positions
  List<Vector2> newPositions = new List<Vector2>();

  // Between each control point...
  for (int i = 0; i < positions.Count - 1; i++)
  {
    // Add the control point to the new list
    newPositions.Add(positions[i]);

    // Add the specified number of interpolated points
    for (int j = 0; j < nDivisions; j++)
    {
      // Determine how far to interpolate
      float amt = (float)(j + 1) / (float)(nDivisions + 2);

     // Find the position based on catmull-rom interpolation
      Vector2 interp = catmullRomV2(
        positions[wrapIndex(i - 1, positions.Count - 1)], positions[i],
        positions[wrapIndex(i + 1, positions.Count - 1)],
        positions[wrapIndex(i + 2, positions.Count - 1)], amt);

      // Add the new position to the new list
     newPositions.Add(interp);
    }
  }

  return newPositions;
}


// Wraps a number around 0 and the "max" value
int wrapIndex(int value, int max)
{
  while (value > max)
```

```
        value -= max;
    while (value < 0)
        value += max;

    return value;
}


// Performs a Catmull-Rom interpolation for each component of a
Vector2 based
// on the given control points and interpolation distance
Vector2 catmullRomV2(Vector2 v1, Vector2 v2, Vector2 v3, Vector2 v4,
float amount)
{
    return new Vector2(MathHelper.CatmullRom(v1.X, v2.X, v3.X, v4.X,
amount),
        MathHelper.CatmullRom(v1.Y, v2.Y, v3.Y, v4.Y, amount));
}
```

Having added a number of additional points to the list of track points, we now need to create the vertices and indices to trace a track through them. We add a vertex to the left and right of each track point and create two triangles to fill the space between each track section. We find the side vector by taking the cross product of the forward vector (the vector between the next and the current position) and the up vector (0, 1, 0).

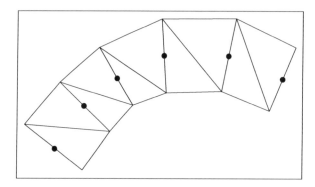

We create the vertices as follows. For the sake of brevity, I won't step through the code in pieces, as it is well commented:

```
VertexPositionNormalTexture[] createVertices(float trackWidth,
    int textureRepetitions)
{
    // Create 2 vertices for each track point
    nVertices = positions.Count * 2;
```

```
VertexPositionNormalTexture[] vertices = new
   VertexPositionNormalTexture[nVertices];

int j = 0;
trackLength = 0;

for (int i = 0; i < positions.Count; i++)
{
  // Find the index of the next position
  int next = wrapIndex(i + 1, positions.Count - 1);

  // Find the current and next positions on the path
  Vector3 position = new Vector3(positions[i].X, 0, positions[i].Y);
  Vector3 nextPosition = new Vector3(positions[next].X, 0,
  positions[next].Y);

  // Find the vector between the current and next position
  Vector3 forward = nextPosition - position;
  float length = forward.Length();
  forward.Normalize();

  // Find the side vector based on the forward and up vectors
  Vector3 side = -Vector3.Cross(forward, Vector3.Up) * trackWidth;

  // Create a vertex to the left and right of the current position
  vertices[j++] = new VertexPositionNormalTexture(position - side,
    Vector3.Up, new Vector2(0, trackLength));
  vertices[j++] = new VertexPositionNormalTexture(position + side,
    Vector3.Up, new Vector2(1, trackLength));

  trackLength += length;
}

// Attach the end vertices to the beginning to close the loop
vertices[vertices.Length - 1].Position = vertices[1].Position;
vertices[vertices.Length - 2].Position = vertices[0].Position;

// For each vertex...
for (int i = 0; i < vertices.Length; i++)
{
  // Bring the UV's Y coordinate back to the [0, 1] range
  vertices[i].TextureCoordinate.Y /= trackLength;
```

```
    // Tile the texture along the track
    vertices[i].TextureCoordinate.Y *= textureRepetitions;
  }

  return vertices;
}
```

Next, we need to create the indices. All we need to do is create two triangles between each track position:

```
int[] createIndices()
{
  // Create indices
  nIndices = (positions.Count - 1) * 6;
  int[] indices = new int[nIndices];

  int j = 0;

  // Create two triangles between every position
  for (int i = 0; i < positions.Count - 1; i++)
  {
    int i0 = i * 2;

    indices[j++] = i0;
    indices[j++] = i0 + 1;
    indices[j++] = i0 + 2;
    indices[j++] = i0 + 2;
    indices[j++] = i0 + 1;
    indices[j++] = i0 + 3;
  }

  return indices;
}
```

The `createBuffers()` function ties the vertex and index creation together:

```
void createBuffers(float trackWidth, int textureRepetitions)
{
  VertexPositionNormalTexture[] vertices = createVertices(trackWidth,
    textureRepetitions);

  // Create vertex buffer and set data
  vb = new VertexBuffer(graphicsDevice,
      typeof(VertexPositionNormalTexture),
      vertices.Length, BufferUsage.WriteOnly);
```

```
    vb.SetData<VertexPositionNormalTexture>(vertices);
    int[] indices = createIndices();

    // Create index buffer and set data
    ib = new IndexBuffer(graphicsDevice, IndexElementSize.ThirtyTwoBits,
        indices.Length, BufferUsage.WriteOnly);
    ib.SetData<int>(indices);
}
```

Drawing the track is very simple:

```
public void Draw(Matrix View, Matrix Projection)
{
  // Set effect parameters
  effect.World = Matrix.Identity;
  effect.View = View;
  effect.Projection = Projection;
  effect.Texture = texture;
  effect.TextureEnabled = true;

  // Set the vertex and index buffers to the graphics device
  graphicsDevice.SetVertexBuffer(vb);
  graphicsDevice.Indices = ib;

  // Apply the effect
  effect.CurrentTechnique.Passes[0].Apply();

  // Draw the list of triangles
  graphicsDevice.DrawIndexedPrimitives(PrimitiveType.TriangleList,
     0, 0, nVertices, 0, nIndices / 3);
}
```

Let's now create a track in our game:

```
RaceTrack track;
```

We initialize it as follows in the LoadContent() function:

```
List<Vector2> trackPositions = new List<Vector2>()
{
  new Vector2(-4000, 0),
  new Vector2(-4000, -4000),
  new Vector2(0, -4000),
  new Vector2(4000, -4000),
```

```
    new Vector2(4000, -2000),
    new Vector2(0, -2000),
    new Vector2(-1000, 0),
    new Vector2(0, 2000),
    new Vector2(4000, 2000),
    new Vector2(4000, 4000),
    new Vector2(0, 4000),
    new Vector2(-4000, 4000),
    new Vector2(-4000, 0)
};

track = new RaceTrack(trackPositions, 25, 300, 30, GraphicsDevice,
Content);
```

Finally, we draw the terrain as follows:

```
track.Draw(camera.View, camera.Projection);
```

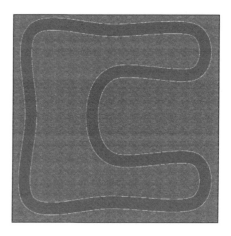

Moving a car along the track

Now that we can create and render our race track, we are ready to add a car to our little racing game. First, we will need a way to determine where on the track the car is, based on a distance value. This function will be able to handle the car looping around the track, and will be able to interpolate between track positions:

```
// Returns the position on the track the given distance from the start,
// and the forward direction at that point
public Vector2 TracePath(float distance, out Vector2 direction)
{
  // Remove extra laps
  while (distance > trackLength)
    distance -= trackLength;

  int i = 0;

  while (true)
  {
    // Find the index of the next and last position
    int last = wrapIndex(i - 1, positions.Count - 1);
    int next = wrapIndex(i + 1, positions.Count - 1);

    // Find the distance between this position and the next
    direction = positions[next] - positions[i];
    float length = direction.Length();

    // If the length remaining is greater than the distance to
    // the next position, keep looping. Otherwise, the
    // final position is somewhere between the current and next
    // position in the list
    if (length < distance)
    {
      distance -= length;
      i++;
      continue;
    }

    // Find the direction from the last position to the current
    //   position
    Vector2 lastDirection = positions[i] - positions[last];
    lastDirection.Normalize();
    direction.Normalize();

    // Determine how far the position is between the current and next
    // positions in the list
    float amt = distance / length;
```

```
        // Interpolate the last and current direction and current and
        // next position to find final direction and position
        direction = Vector2.Lerp(lastDirection, direction, amt);
        return Vector2.Lerp(positions[i], positions[next], amt);
    }
}
```

Now we are ready to animate the car. First, we load the car as usual. In this case, the car is filling the second position in the list as the ground is loaded into the first position.

```
models.Add(new CModel(Content.Load<Model>("car"), Vector3.Zero,
    Vector3.Zero, Vector3.One, GraphicsDevice));
```

We'll attach a chase camera to the car:

```
camera = new ChaseCamera(new Vector3(0, 250, 700),
    new Vector3(0, 250, 0),
    new Vector3(0, MathHelper.Pi, 0), GraphicsDevice);
```

The camera will need to be updated at the very end of the Update() function:

```
((ChaseCamera)camera).Move(models[1].Position, models[1].Rotation);
((ChaseCamera)camera).Update();
```

We will also need to update the references in the Draw() function to treat the camera as a ChaseCamera instead of a FreeCamera:

```
foreach (CModel model in models)
  if (camera.BoundingVolumeIsInView(model.BoundingSphere))
    model.Draw(camera.View, camera.Projection, ((ChaseCamera)camera).
Position);

track.Draw(camera.View, camera.Projection);
```

To make things more interesting, we will simulate some simple velocity/acceleration physics on our car. We will need distance and speed values:

```
float distance = 0;
float speed = 0;
```

We will work with these values at the beginning of the Update() function:

```
// Update the car speed for acceleration, braking, and friction
if (Keyboard.GetState().IsKeyDown(Keys.Up))
  speed += 1000 * (float)gameTime.ElapsedGameTime.TotalSeconds;
else if (Keyboard.GetState().IsKeyDown(Keys.Down))
  speed -= 2500 * (float)gameTime.ElapsedGameTime.TotalSeconds;
else
```

```
speed -= 1500 * (float)gameTime.ElapsedGameTime.TotalSeconds;

// Limit the speed min/max
speed = MathHelper.Clamp(speed, 0, 2000);

// Increase the distance based on speed
distance += speed * (float)gameTime.ElapsedGameTime.TotalSeconds;
```

Next, we get the position and direction of the car from the race track based on our distance value, and move the car accordingly:

```
// Get position and direction of car from track class
Vector2 direction;
Vector2 trackPosition = track.TracePath(distance, out direction);

// Convert direction vector to angle
float rotation = (float)Math.Acos(direction.Y > 0 ? -direction.X :
direction.X);

if (direction.Y > 0)
  rotation += MathHelper.Pi;

rotation += MathHelper.PiOver2;

// Move and rotate car accordingly
models[1].Position = new Vector3(trackPosition.X, 20, trackPosition.Y);
models[1].Rotation = new Vector3(0, rotation, 0);
```

Running the game, you can drive the car using the *up* key to accelerate and the *back* key to brake. Also notice that with no input the car will slow down by itself due to friction.

Hierarchical animation

Thus far, we have looked at animation of objects as a whole, but this is interesting only to a point. Next, we'll look at **hierarchical animation**—animation of individual parts of a model. We call it hierarchical animation because models are generally built as a hierarchy of pieces, where transforming one piece will also affect its children. For example, a windmill may have the following hierarchy:

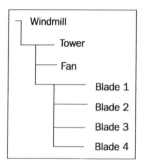

If we were to rotate the **Fan** part of the hierarchy, you can see that each blade would also be rotated. Let's try this in our game. First, we load the windmill and an animation:

```
models.Add(new CModel(Content.Load<Model>("windmill"),
    Vector3.Zero, Vector3.Zero, new Vector3(0.25f), GraphicsDevice));

anim = new ObjectAnimation(new Vector3(0, 875, 0),
        new Vector3(0, 875, 0),
    Vector3.Zero, new Vector3(0, 0, MathHelper.TwoPi),
    TimeSpan.FromSeconds(10), true);
```

This animation will simply rotate the fan blade in a circle every ten seconds. Now, all we need to do is link the animation to the **Fan** mesh in the Update() function, and the fan will spin independently of the tower. Because the fan is spinning, the blades will spin as well, as they are linked hierarchically to the **Fan** piece:

```
models[0].Model.Meshes["Fan"].ParentBone.Transform =
  Matrix.CreateRotationZ(anim.Rotation.Z) *
    Matrix.CreateTranslation(anim.Position);
```

We will revisit hierarchical animation when we get to skinned models, but for any "normal" (non-skinned) model—like those we have been using throughout the book—simply manipulating the bone transforms, like we did earlier, will be enough to perform most animations of individual pieces of a model.

Skinned animation

The final type of animation we will look at is skinned animation. **Skinned animation** animates the individual vertices of an object based on the object's skeleton. Each bone is assigned a number of vertices, which it will affect when moved. For each of those vertices, each bone is also assigned a weight determining how much influence the bone will have on each vertex. This technique is especially useful for animating characters, animals, and so on, because it makes it easy to simulate a smooth, flowing, morphing skin with a skeleton inside. For example, it is easy to model an arm as being made up of a few bones, which will deform the skin when moved. This makes for a much more realistic effect than other approaches and makes animation easy because the animator only has to worry about animating the bones of a character—the skinning process will take care of animating each individual vertex.

Skinned animation also commonly makes use of keyframed animation: animators will specify positions and orientations for each bone at specific frames and allow the interpolation functions to handle the frames between the key frames. To make matters even simpler (building off of even more of what we have learned), the bones of a model are almost always modeled as a hierarchy, so transformations of one bone will be reflected by its children. For example, moving a character's thigh will also move its lower leg and foot, without any extra animation needed.

Before we can render skinned models, we need to be able to load them. XNA doesn't provide a content processor for the content pipeline to build and load a skinned model. Therefore, we will need to write our own. We will base this off of the skinned model sample available at apphub.com. To begin with, we need to add a few projects to our game's solution. We will need two new projects—a neutral class library to store classes that can be accessed by the content pipeline and the game, and the content pipeline extension itself. To add a new project, right-click on the solution in the **Solution Explorer** in Visual Studio (labeled **Solution MyGame** (two projects)) and click on **Add New Project**. We will do this twice—adding a **Windows Game Library** called SkinnedModel the first time, and a **Content Pipeline Extension Library** called SkinnedModelPipeline the second time.

We now need to link all of the projects together so that each project will have access to what they need to build. The game and content pipeline extension will need access to the SkinnedModel project, and the game's content project will need access to the content pipeline extension. In the **Solution Explorer**, first right-click on **References** under the **Content Pipeline Extension** project (SkinnedModelPipeline) and under **Projects** in the pop-up window, choose SkinnedModel. Do the same for the MyGame project. Add a reference in the MyGameContent project to the SkinnedModelPipeline project.

We will need a few classes in the SkinnedModel project for animation. First, we will need a somewhat familiar Keyframe class. This class stores the transformation of a single bone as a matrix, the index of the bone the keyframe stores the transformation of, and the time from the beginning of the animation of the keyframe:

```
public class Keyframe
{
  // Index of the bone this keyframe animates
  [ContentSerializer]
  public int Bone { get; private set; }

  // Time from the beginning of the animation of this keyframe
  [ContentSerializer]
  public TimeSpan Time { get; private set; }

  // Bone transform for this keyframe
  [ContentSerializer]
  public Matrix Transform { get; private set; }

  public Keyframe(int Bone, TimeSpan Time, Matrix Transform)
  {
    this.Bone = Bone;
    this.Time = Time;
```

```
    this.Transform = Transform;
  }

  private Keyframe()
  {
  }
}
```

The ContentSerializer attribute on the public properties and the blank constructor of this class will allow the content pipeline to serialize the class so that it can be recreated when loaded by the game. Next, the AnimationClip class stores all of the keyframes for all of the bones of an animation:

```
public class AnimationClip
{
  // Total length of the clip
  [ContentSerializer]
  public TimeSpan Duration { get; private set; }

  // List of keyframes for all bones, sorted by time
  [ContentSerializer]
  public List<Keyframe> Keyframes { get; private set; }

  public AnimationClip(TimeSpan Duration, List<Keyframe> Keyframes)
  {
    this.Duration = Duration;
    this.Keyframes = Keyframes;
  }

  private AnimationClip()
  {
  }
}
```

Finally, the SkinningData class stores all of the data needed to load, animate, and draw a skinned model. First, it stores all of the animation clips a model may happen to contain. Next, it contains the matrix transformations for each bone (relative to their parent's bone) that will put the model in what is called its "bind pose"—the "default" pose of the model. The SkinningData class also contains the inverse matrices of the bind pose matrices, to convert back from the bind pose. Finally, this class stores the skeleton hierarchy of the model by storing the parent index of each bone:

```
public class SkinningData
{
  // Gets a collection of animation clips, stored by name
  [ContentSerializer]
```

```
    public Dictionary<string, AnimationClip> AnimationClips { get;
private set; }

    // Bind pose matrices for each bone in the skeleton,
    // relative to the parent bone.
    [ContentSerializer]
    public List<Matrix> BindPose { get; private set; }

    // Vertex to bonespace transforms for each bone in the skeleton.
    [ContentSerializer]
    public List<Matrix> InverseBindPose { get; private set; }

    // For each bone in the skeleton, stores the index of the parent bone.
    [ContentSerializer]
    public List<int> SkeletonHierarchy { get; private set; }

    public SkinningData(Dictionary<string, AnimationClip>
animationClips,
      List<Matrix> bindPose, List<Matrix> inverseBindPose,
      List<int> skeletonHierarchy)
    {
      AnimationClips = animationClips;
      BindPose = bindPose;
      InverseBindPose = inverseBindPose;
      SkeletonHierarchy = skeletonHierarchy;
    }

    private SkinningData()
    {
    }
}
```

Loading a skinned model

In XNA, the content pipeline is responsible for processing content files—models, textures, and so on—and converting them into a format that is ready to be loaded by the game. The content pipeline is a two stage process—first, content is run through an **importer** that converts files of the same type (.fbx and .x models, or .jpg and .png and .tga textures, for example) to the same intermediate format. This intermediate data is then further processed by a content processor. The **content processor** is responsible for taking the data provided by the importer and creating an object that can be serialized (saved to a file) and loaded directly by the game's content manager. In this case, we will take the animation data that has been loaded by the importer and create a SkinningData object attached to the regular model output by the content processor.

With these three classes, we are ready to write the content processor that will process the model file. XNA's model importer will have already extracted the data from the model file, so all we need to do is extract the data that we need and convert it to a format we can use. We will do this in the SkinnedModelPipeline project, with a processor called SkinnedModelProcessor:

```
[DisplayName("Skinned Model Processor")]
public class SkinnedModelProcessor : ModelProcessor
{
}
```

The Process() function is primarily responsible for converting the data we are given to the format we desire:

```
public override ModelContent Process(NodeContent input,
    ContentProcessorContext context)
{
}
```

The first step is to find the skeleton of the model in the data we are given, by using the MeshHelper.FindSkeleton() function. We then extract the bones from that skeleton using the same class' FlattenSkeleton() function:

```
// Find the skeleton.
BoneContent skeleton = MeshHelper.FindSkeleton(input);

// Read the bind pose and skeleton hierarchy data.
IList<BoneContent> bones = MeshHelper.FlattenSkeleton(skeleton);
```

Next, we will extract the bind post matrix transformations from the bones as well as the hierarchy of the parent bone indices:

```
List<Matrix> bindPose = new List<Matrix>();
List<Matrix> inverseBindPose = new List<Matrix>();
List<int> skeletonHierarchy = new List<int>();

// Extract the bind pose transform, inverse bind pose transform,
// and parent bone index of each bone in order
foreach (BoneContent bone in bones)
{
  bindPose.Add(bone.Transform);
  inverseBindPose.Add(Matrix.Invert(bone.AbsoluteTransform));
  skeletonHierarchy.Add(bones.IndexOf(bone.Parent as BoneContent));
}
```

The next step is to process all of the animations in the model. We will do this with a
function called `ProcessAnimations()`, which we will write in a moment:

```
// Convert animation data to our runtime format.
Dictionary<string, AnimationClip> animationClips;
animationClips = ProcessAnimations(skeleton.Animations, bones);
```

Once we have processed all of this data, we call the `base.Process()` function so that
the `Process()` function of the default `ModelProcessor` can process the rest of the
data contained in the model (including the bone weights). Then we create an instance
of the `SkinningData` class, fill it with all of the data we collected, and set it as the
model's tag:

```
// Chain to the base ModelProcessor class so it can convert the model
data.
ModelContent model = base.Process(input, context);

// Store our custom animation data in the Tag property of the model.
model.Tag = new SkinningData(animationClips, bindPose,
inverseBindPose,
    skeletonHierarchy);

return model;
```

The content importer will have provided the animations of the model as an
`AnimationContentDictionary` object, so the `ProcessAnimations()` function's
job is to convert that object into our `AnimationClip` object. We do this by first
building a dictionary of bone names and indices. Next, we process all of the
individual animations in the dictionary. Finally, we add each animation to a
dictionary of animation clips. The table of bone names and indices is needed by the
`ProcessAnimation()` function to convert between bone names and indices when
processing a single animation:

```
static Dictionary<string, AnimationClip> ProcessAnimations(
  AnimationContentDictionary animations, IList<BoneContent> bones)
{
  // Build up a table mapping bone names to indices.
  Dictionary<string, int> boneMap = new Dictionary<string, int>();

  for (int i = 0; i < bones.Count; i++)
    boneMap.Add(bones[i].Name, i);

  Dictionary<string, AnimationClip> animationClips =
    new Dictionary<string, AnimationClip>();

  // Convert each animation
```

```
    foreach (KeyValuePair<string, AnimationContent> animation in
animations)
    {
        AnimationClip processed = ProcessAnimation(animation.Value,
boneMap);
        animationClips.Add(animation.Key, processed);
    }

    return animationClips;
}
```

The `ProcessAnimation()` function is responsible for taking a single animation from the `AnimationContentDictionary` (stored as an `AnimationContent` object) and converting it into an `AnimationClip`, filled with keyframes. It does this by looking at each animation channel in the animation. An **animation channel** contains all of the key frames for one bone of a model. This function, then, needs to determine what bone the animation channel controls, and extract all of the key frames in the animation channel. Finally, having loaded all of the key frames for each bone, the `ProcessAnimation()` function sorts all of the key frames by their time in the animation using a comparison function:

```
static AnimationClip ProcessAnimation(AnimationContent animation,
    Dictionary<string, int> boneMap)
{
    List<Keyframe> keyframes = new List<Keyframe>();

    // For each input animation channel.
    foreach (KeyValuePair<string, AnimationChannel> channel in
        animation.Channels)
    {
        // Look up what bone this channel is controlling.
        int boneIndex = boneMap[channel.Key];

        // Convert the keyframe data.
        foreach (AnimationKeyframe keyframe in channel.Value)
            keyframes.Add(new Keyframe(boneIndex, keyframe.Time,
            keyframe.Transform));
    }

    // Sort the merged keyframes by time.
    keyframes.Sort(CompareKeyframeTimes);

    return new AnimationClip(animation.Duration, keyframes);
}
```

```
static int CompareKeyframeTimes(Keyframe a, Keyframe b)
{
    return a.Time.CompareTo(b.Time);
}
```

We can now build a model using our content processor and load it into the game. We'll use the `dude.fbx` model from the skinning sample (also included in the code download). To build the model with the correct content processor, we need to tell XNA to use the **Skinned Model Processor** by right-clicking on the model in the **Solution Explorer**, opening its properties, and setting the `Content Processor` property to the previously mentioned value:

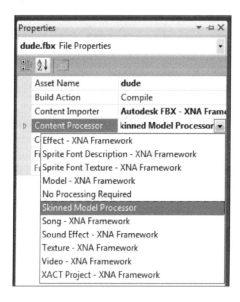

In order to render a skinned model, we need to use an `Effect` that will perform the vertex transformations based on bone transformations. XNA provides a built-in effect called `SkinnedEffect` that can do this for us. Let's create a new class that will handle skinned models for us:

```
public class SkinnedModel
{
    Model model;
    GraphicsDevice graphicsDevice;
    ContentManager content;

    SkinningData skinningData;

    public Vector3 Position, Rotation, Scale;
```

```
public Model Model { get { return model; } }

public SkinnedModel(Model Model, Vector3 Position, Vector3 Rotation,
    Vector3 Scale, GraphicsDevice GraphicsDevice,
    ContentManager Content)
{
  this.model = Model;
  this.graphicsDevice = GraphicsDevice;
  this.content = Content;
  this.Position = Position;
  this.Rotation = Rotation;
  this.Scale = Scale;

  this.skinningData = model.Tag as SkinningData;

  setNewEffect();
  }
}
```

The setNewEffect() function changes the effect used by the model to a SkinnedEffect and copies the texture, diffuse color, and so on from the old effect to the new effect:

```
void setNewEffect()
{
  foreach (ModelMesh mesh in model.Meshes)
  {
    foreach (ModelMeshPart part in mesh.MeshParts)
    {
      SkinnedEffect newEffect = new SkinnedEffect(graphicsDevice);
      BasicEffect oldEffect = ((BasicEffect)part.Effect);

      newEffect.EnableDefaultLighting();
      newEffect.SpecularColor = Color.Black.ToVector3();

      newEffect.AmbientLightColor = oldEffect.AmbientLightColor;
      newEffect.DiffuseColor = oldEffect.DiffuseColor;
      newEffect.Texture = oldEffect.Texture;

      part.Effect = newEffect;
    }
  }
}
```

Finally, the `Draw()` function draws the model as usual:

```
public void Draw(Matrix View, Matrix Projection, Vector3
CameraPosition)
{
  Matrix world = Matrix.CreateScale(Scale) *
    Matrix.CreateFromYawPitchRoll(Rotation.Y, Rotation.X, Rotation.Z) *
    Matrix.CreateTranslation(Position);

  foreach (ModelMesh mesh in model.Meshes)
  {
    foreach (SkinnedEffect effect in mesh.Effects)
    {
      effect.World = world;
      effect.View = View;
      effect.Projection = Projection;
    }

    mesh.Draw();
  }
}
```

Right now, this class may not seem complicated enough to be warranted, but we will see in a moment why we created a separate `SkinnedModel` class. We can test it at this most basic level right now, by creating an instance of this class in our game:

```
SkinnedModel skinnedModel;
```

We initialize it in the `LoadContent()` function just like a `CModel`:

```
skinnedModel = new SkinnedModel(Content.Load<Model>("dude"),
  Vector3.Zero,new Vector3(0, MathHelper.Pi, 0), new Vector3(10),
  GraphicsDevice, Content);
```

We also draw it just like a `CModel`:

```
skinnedModel.Draw(camera.View, camera.Projection,
((FreeCamera)camera).Position);
```

Running the game, we should see the model in its bind pose. The model will be facing backwards without an animation playing if you use the `dude.fbx` model. This will change when an animation plays.

Playing a skinned animation

In order to play a skinned animation, we need to, for each frame, find the transformations to be applied to each bone according to the current keyframe of the animation. The `Effect` will then take those transformations and use them to move the vertices of our model. We will use XNA's `SkinnedEffect` to perform the second function. However, to perform the first function of determining the current keyframe and determining what the bone transformations should be, we will create a new class—`AnimationPlayer`.

```
public class AnimationPlayer
{
  SkinningData skinningData;

  // The currently playing clip, if there is one
  public AnimationClip CurrentClip { get; private set; }

  // Whether the current animation has finished
  public bool Done { get; private set; }

  // Timing values
  TimeSpan startTime, endTime, currentTime;
  bool loop;
  int currentKeyframe;

  // Transforms
  public Matrix[] BoneTransforms { get; private set; }
  public Matrix[] WorldTransforms { get; private set; }
  public Matrix[] SkinTransforms { get; private set; }
```

```
        public AnimationPlayer(SkinningData skinningData)
        {
            this.skinningData = skinningData;

            BoneTransforms = new Matrix[skinningData.BindPose.Count];
            WorldTransforms = new Matrix[skinningData.BindPose.Count];
            SkinTransforms = new Matrix[skinningData.BindPose.Count];
        }
    }
```

The `AnimationPlayer` class will be responsible for playing back animation clips. It would be nice if all of the separate animations included in a model were stored as individual animation clips, but unfortunately, many modeling packages export only a single `AnimationClip`, with all of the animations placed together in a sequence. For this reason, we want to be able to playback only a specific portion of an `AnimationClip`. To accommodate this, we will provide a number of overloads for the `StartClip()` function, which is responsible for resetting the animation player and getting ready to play a given `AnimationClip`:

```
// Starts playing the entirety of the given clip
public void StartClip(string clip, bool loop)
{
    AnimationClip clipVal = skinningData.AnimationClips[clip];
    StartClip(clip, TimeSpan.FromSeconds(0), clipVal.Duration, loop);
}


// Plays a specific portion of the given clip, from one frame
// index to another
public void StartClip(string clip, int startFrame, int endFrame,
    bool loop)
{
    AnimationClip clipVal = skinningData.AnimationClips[clip];

    StartClip(clip, clipVal.Keyframes[startFrame].Time,
        clipVal.Keyframes[endFrame].Time, loop);
}


// Plays a specific portion of the given clip, from one time
// to another
public void StartClip(string clip, TimeSpan StartTime,
    TimeSpan EndTime, bool loop)
{
    CurrentClip = skinningData.AnimationClips[clip];
    currentTime = TimeSpan.FromSeconds(0);
```

```
    currentKeyframe = 0;
    Done = false;
    this.startTime = StartTime;
    this.endTime = EndTime;
    this.loop = loop;

    // Copy the bind pose to the bone transforms array to reset the
    // animation
    skinningData.BindPose.CopyTo(BoneTransforms, 0);
}
```

The `Update()` function increases the time value, then updates the three arrays of transformations:

```
public void Update(TimeSpan time, Matrix rootTransform)
{
    if (CurrentClip == null || Done)
        return;

    currentTime += time;

    updateBoneTransforms();
    updateWorldTransforms(rootTransform);
    updateSkinTransforms();
}
```

First, we update the bone transforms:

```
// Helper used by the Update method to refresh the BoneTransforms data
void updateBoneTransforms()
{
    // If the current time has passed the end of the animation...
    while (currentTime >= (endTime - startTime))
    {
        // If we are looping, reduce the time until we are
        // back in the animation's time frame
        if (loop)
        {
            currentTime -= (endTime - startTime);
            currentKeyframe = 0;
            skinningData.BindPose.CopyTo(BoneTransforms, 0);
        }
        // Otherwise, clamp to the end of the animation
        else
        {
            Done = true;
```

```
        currentTime = endTime;
        break;
      }
   }


   // Read keyframe matrices
   IList<Keyframe> keyframes = CurrentClip.Keyframes;

   // Read keyframes until we have found the latest frame before
   // the current time
   while (currentKeyframe < keyframes.Count)
   {
      Keyframe keyframe = keyframes[currentKeyframe];

      // Stop when we've read up to the current time position.
      if (keyframe.Time > currentTime + startTime)
         break;

      // Use this keyframe.
      BoneTransforms[keyframe.Bone] = keyframe.Transform;

      currentKeyframe++;
   }
}
```

Next, we update the world transforms. This will give us the world space transformation of each bone, including its parent transform:

```
// Helper used by the Update method to refresh the WorldTransforms
data
void updateWorldTransforms(Matrix rootTransform)
{
  // Root bone
  WorldTransforms[0] = BoneTransforms[0] * rootTransform;

  // For each child bone...
  for (int bone = 1; bone < WorldTransforms.Length; bone++)
  {
     // Add the transform of the parent bone
     int parentBone = skinningData.SkeletonHierarchy[bone];

     WorldTransforms[bone] = BoneTransforms[bone] *
         WorldTransforms[parentBone];
  }
}
```

Finally, we can update the skin transforms. These are the matrices actually used to render the model:

```
// Helper used by the Update method to refresh the SkinTransforms data
void updateSkinTransforms()
{
   for (int bone = 0; bone < SkinTransforms.Length; bone++)
       SkinTransforms[bone] = skinningData.InverseBindPose[bone] *
          WorldTransforms[bone];
}
```

We can now update the `SkinnedModel` class to use an `AnimationPlayer` to play animations:

```
public SkinnedAnimationPlayer Player { get; private set; }
```

We initialize this player in the constructor:

```
this.skinningData = model.Tag as SkinningData;
Player = new SkinnedAnimationPlayer(skinningData);
```

Next, we add an `Update()` function that will update the player and perform the world matrix calculation:

```
public void Update(GameTime gameTime)
{
  Matrix world = Matrix.CreateScale(Scale) *
      Matrix.CreateFromYawPitchRoll(Rotation.Y, Rotation.X, Rotation.Z) *
      Matrix.CreateTranslation(Position);

  Player.Update(gameTime.ElapsedGameTime, world);
}
```

Finally, we can update the `draw` function to set the skin transforms from the animation player to the `SkinnedEffect` attached to each `MeshPart`:

```
public void Draw(Matrix View, Matrix Projection, Vector3
CameraPosition)
{
  foreach (ModelMesh mesh in model.Meshes)
  {
     foreach (SkinnedEffect effect in mesh.Effects)
     {
       effect.SetBoneTransforms(Player.SkinTransforms);
       effect.View = View;
```

```
        effect.Projection = Projection;
    }

    mesh.Draw();
    }
}
```

Back in the `Game1` class, we must be sure to call the skinned model's `update` function:

```
skinnedModel.Update(gameTime);
```

Finally, we can play this character's walking animation by calling the `StartClip()` function of the `AnimationPlayer` of the `SkinnedModel`:

```
skinnedModel.Player.StartClip("Take 001", true);
```

Changing an animation's play speed

With the `SkinnedModel` class set up the way it is, it would be very easy to change the speed at which its animations are played. All we need to do is lie to the `AnimationPlayer` about how much time has elapsed between frames. First, we'll add a `PlaySpeed` property:

```
public float PlaySpeed = 1.0f;
```

We can then modify the `Update()` function to use a modified elapsed time when updating the `AnimationPlayer`:

```
TimeSpan elapsedTime = TimeSpan.FromSeconds(
    gameTime.ElapsedGameTime.TotalSeconds * PlaySpeed);

Player.Update(elapsedTime, world);
```

We could make our character walk in slow motion, then, by changing the `PlaySpeed` property:

```
skinnedModel.PlaySpeed = 0.5f;
```

Model attachments

A very useful trick when animating models, or when drawing models in general, is attaching models to certain parts of other models. In the next example, we will attach a gun model to the hand of our "dude" model. The first step is to find the index of the bone controlling the hand. We will store that index in a variable. We will have to load our model as a regular `Model` instead of the `CModel`, so that we can set the world matrix directly:

```
Model gun;
int handIndex;
```

We find the index of the hand through the `Model` class of the underlying `SkinnedModel`, while loading the `gun` model:

```
gun = Content.Load<Model>("mp5");

foreach(ModelMesh mesh in gun.Meshes)
  foreach (BasicEffect effect in mesh.Effects)
  {
     effect.Texture = Content.Load<Texture2D>("mp5_tex");
     effect.TextureEnabled = true;
     effect.EnableDefaultLighting();
  }

handIndex = skinnedModel.Model.Bones["R_Hand"].Index;
```

We can now draw the `gun` model as follows, applying both a transformation to make the gun model lineup with the character's hand and the world transformation of the character's hand itself:

```
foreach (ModelMesh mesh in gun.Meshes)
{
  foreach (BasicEffect effect in mesh.Effects)
  {
    Matrix gunTransform = Matrix.CreateScale(0.65f) *
        Matrix.CreateFromYawPitchRoll(-MathHelper.PiOver2, 0,
        MathHelper.Pi);

    effect.World = gunTransform *
                   skinnedModel.Player.WorldTransforms[handIndex];
```

```
        effect.View = camera.View;
        effect.Projection = camera.Projection;
    }

    mesh.Draw();
}
```

Summary

Having completed this chapter, you have learned about several different types
of animation—you have learned how to animate objects as a whole with some
very simple position and rotation interpolation and interpolation over a curve.
You have also learned how to create a race track from a curve and how to move
a car along that path and track. You have also learned about hierarchical
animation—the animation of an object's skeleton and submeshes. You also
learned about "keyframed" animation, and how to create more complex
animations using it. Finally, you learned about "skinned" animation:
animation of the individual vertices of a model according to the model's
skeleton's transformations.

Index

Symbols

3D coordinate system 10

A

AddParticle() function 172
advanced materials 206-208
A key 24
AlphaTestValue parameter 158
ambient lighting 56, 57
amt argument 238
animation
  keyframed animation 233, 234
  object animation 231
  play speed, changing 266
  skinned animation 251, 252
  skinned animation, playing 261
  Update() function 266
animation channel 257
AnimationClip class 253
AnimationContentDictionary object 256
AnimationPlayer class, creating 261, 262
anisotropic filtering 55
arc-ball camera
  about 31
  ArcBall Camera class 32, 33
  LoadContent() method 34
ArcBall Camera class 32, 33
aspect ratio 15

B

base.Draw() 224
base.Process() function 256
BasicEffect 15, 66

BasicTexture parameter 52
Billboarding 149
Billboards
  drawing 153-156
  non-rotating 163-166
BillboardSystem 196, 198
billboard system
  adding, to render clouds 200-203
BillboardSystem class
  about 156, 159, 164
  creating 150, 152
black and white post processor 212, 213
BoundingFrustum class 29
BoundingSphere member variable 27
bounding spheres
  calculating, for models 27, 28
boundingSphere value 28
bounding volume 27
buildBoundingSphere() 45

C

CachedEffect variable 45
camera
  arc-ball camera 31, 34
  chase camera 34-36
  types 31, 34
  upgrading, to free camera 24-27
Camera base class 21
Camera class
  creating 21, 22
Catmull-Rom interpolation
  about 237
  amt argument 238
  KeyframedObjectAnimation class,
    modifying 238

VSM
about 110
benefits 110
depth texture, blurring 111-114
shadows, generating 115, 116
soft shadows, implementing 110

W

WaterEffect class 146
W key 24
world matrix 11
world space 11
wrap() function 238

X

XNA game project
setting up 7-9

Z

Z-axis 10

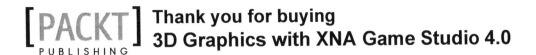

About Packt Publishing

Packt, pronounced 'packed', published its first book "*Mastering phpMyAdmin for Effective MySQL Management*" in April 2004 and subsequently continued to specialize in publishing highly focused books on specific technologies and solutions.

Our books and publications share the experiences of your fellow IT professionals in adapting and customizing today's systems, applications, and frameworks. Our solution based books give you the knowledge and power to customize the software and technologies you're using to get the job done. Packt books are more specific and less general than the IT books you have seen in the past. Our unique business model allows us to bring you more focused information, giving you more of what you need to know, and less of what you don't.

Packt is a modern, yet unique publishing company, which focuses on producing quality, cutting-edge books for communities of developers, administrators, and newbies alike. For more information, please visit our website: www.packtpub.com.

Writing for Packt

We welcome all inquiries from people who are interested in authoring. Book proposals should be sent to author@packtpub.com. If your book idea is still at an early stage and you would like to discuss it first before writing a formal book proposal, contact us; one of our commissioning editors will get in touch with you.

We're not just looking for published authors; if you have strong technical skills but no writing experience, our experienced editors can help you develop a writing career, or simply get some additional reward for your expertise.

Unity 3D Game Development by Example: Beginner's Guide

ISBN: 978-1-849690-54-6   Paperback: 384 pages

A seat-of-your-pants manual for building fun, groovy little games quickly

1. Build fun games using the free Unity 3D game engine even if you've never coded before

2. Learn how to "skin" projects to make totally different games from the same file – more games, less effort!

3. Deploy your games to the Internet so that your friends and family can play them

4. Packed with ideas, inspiration, and advice for your own game design and development

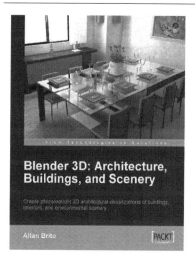

Blender 3D Architecture, Buildings, and Scenery

ISBN: 978-1-847193-67-4   Paperback: 332 pages

Create photorealistic 3D architectural visualizations of buildings, interiors, and environmental scenery

1. Turn your architectural plans into a model

2. Study modeling, materials, textures, and light basics in Blender

3. Create photo-realistic images in detail

4. Create realistic virtual tours of buildings and scenes

Please check **www.PacktPub.com** for information on our titles

Papervision3D Essentials

ISBN: 978-1-847195-72-2   Paperback: 428 pages

Create interactive Papervision 3D applications with stunning effects and powerful animations

1. Build stunning, interactive Papervision3D applications from scratch

2. Export and import 3D models from Autodesk 3ds Max, SketchUp and Blender to Papervision3D

3. In-depth coverage of important 3D concepts with demo applications, screenshots and example code

4. Step-by-step guide for beginners and professionals with tips and tricks based on the authors' practical experience

3D Game Development with Microsoft Silverlight 3: Beginner's Guide

ISBN: 978-1-847198-92-1   Paperback: 452 pages

A practical guide to creating real-time responsive online 3D games in Silverlight 3 using C#, XBAP WPF, XAML, Balder, and Farseer Physics Engine

1. Develop online interactive 3D games and scenes in Microsoft Silverlight 3 and XBAP WPF

2. Integrate Balder 3D engine 1.0, Farseer Physics Engine 2.1, and advanced object-oriented techniques to simplify the game development process

3. Enhance development with animated 3D characters, sounds, music, physics, stages, gauges, and backgrounds

Please check **www.PacktPub.com** for information on our titles